KIT CARSON'S
OWN STORY OF HIS LIFE

Christopher "Kit" Carson

KIT CARSON'S
OWN STORY OF HIS LIFE

Facsimile of Original 1926 Edition

Edited by
Blanche Chloe Grant

With a New Foreword by
Marc Simmons

SOUTHWEST HERITAGE SERIES

SUNSTONE
PRESS

SANTA FE

Sunstone books may be purchased for educational, business, or sales promotional use. For information please write: Special Markets Department, Sunstone Press, P.O. Box 2321, Santa Fe, New Mexico 87504-2321.

Library of Congress Cataloging-in-Publication Data

Carson, Kit, 1809-1868.
    Kit Carson's own story of his life : facsimile of original 1926 edition / edited by Blanche Chloe Grant ; with a new foreword by Marc Simmons.
        p. cm. -- (Southwest heritage series)
    Originally published: Taos, N.M. : [s.n.],1926.
    ISBN 0-86534-568-6 (softcover : alk. paper)
        1. Frontier and pioneer life--West (U.S.) 2. Carson,Kit, 1809-1868.
3. Pioneers--West (U.S.)--Biography. 4. Scouts and scouting--West (U.S.)--Biography.
5. Soldiers--West (U.S.)--Biography. 6. West (U.S.)--Biography. 7. West (U.S.)--
History--To 1848. I. Grant, Blanche C.(Blanche Chloe), 1874-1948. II. Title.

F592.C3 2007
978'.02092--dc22
[B]

                                        2006052282

Published in

WWW.SUNSTONEPRESS.COM
SUNSTONE PRESS / POST OFFICE BOX 2321 / SANTA FE, NM 87504-2321 /USA
(505) 988-4418 / ORDERS ONLY (800) 243-5644 / FAX (505) 988-1025

The Southwest Heritage Series is dedicated to Jody Ellis and Marcia Muth Miller, the founders of Sunstone Press, whose original purpose and vision continues to inspire and motivate our publications.

CONTENTS

I

THE SOUTHWEST HERITAGE SERIES

T he history of the United States is written in hundreds of regional histories and literary works. Those letters, essays, memoirs, biographies and even collections of fiction are often first-hand accounts by people who wanted to memorialize an event, a person or simply record for posterity the concerns and issues of the times. Many of these accounts have been lost, destroyed or overlooked. Some are in private or public collections but deemed to be in too fragile condition to permit handling by contemporary readers and researchers.

However, now with the application of twenty-first century technology, nineteenth and twentieth century material can be reprinted and made accessible to the general public. These early writings are the DNA of our history and culture and are essential to understanding the present in terms of the past.

The Southwest Heritage Series is a form of literary preservation. Heritage by definition implies legacy and these early works are our legacy from those who have gone before us. To properly present and preserve that legacy, no changes in style or contents have been made. The material reprinted stands on its own as it first appeared. The point of view is that of the author and the era in which he or she lived. We would not expect photographs of people from the past to be re-imaged with modern clothes, hair styles and backgrounds. We should not, therefore, expect their ideas and personal philosophies to reflect our modern concepts.

Remember, reading their words and sharing their thoughts is a passport back into understanding how the past was shaped and how it influenced today's world.

Our hope is that new access to these older books will provide readers with a challenging and exciting experience.

Christopher "Kit" Carson

II

FOREWORD TO THIS EDITION
by
Marc Simmons

In 1826 a seventeen-year-old Christopher "Kit" Carson ran away from his job as apprentice to a saddler in Franklin, Missouri and joined a merchant caravan bound for Santa Fe in the far Southwest. The flight marked his entry into the pages of history.

In the decades that followed, Carson gained renown as a trapper, hunter, guide, rancher, army courier, Indian agent, and military officer. Along the way, his varied career as a frontiersman elevated him to the status of a national hero, on a par with Daniel Boone.

In 1856, while at home with his family in Taos, New Mexico, Kit (being illiterate) dictated his autobiography, which dealt with the innumerable adventures he had experienced to that point. However, some of the most significant episodes in his life would unfold in the ensuing years, leading up to his death in 1868.

Since Taos artist and writer Blanche Chloe Grant first edited and published the Carson manuscript in 1926, it has become the central source for all subsequent biographers. In 1935 Milo Milton Quaife annotated another edition under the title of *Kit Carson's Autobiography*, published by Lakeside Press of Chicago, and afterward reprinted by the University of Nebraska Press. Western historian Harvey Lewis Carter followed suit with publication of the most heavily edited version yet, with his *"Dear Old Kit": The Historical Christopher Carson* (Norman: University of Oklahoma Press, 1968).

Sunstone Press by electing to bring back into print Miss Grant's original 1926 book, regarded perhaps as the handiest of the three published versions, calls attention anew to this pioneering memoir of the celebrated Kit Carson.

Grant's *Kit Carson's Own Story of His Life* contains two final chapters added by the editor. Both summarize positive assessments of Carson by people who knew and in some cases worked closely with him.

Also of interest in this reprint edition are the historical photographs, some of which are available nowhere else. They were collected by Grant for inclusion here, and afterward the originals were dispersed and in some cases lost.

Worthy of note are the three photographs of "Col." Dick Rutledge that appear opposite pages 16, 40, and 132. In her captions, Miss Grant refers to him as the last of the old scouts who knew Carson. Today, it is known that Rutledge was one of several elderly impostors who in the early 20th century fraudulently represented themselves as a friend of Kit Carson. Blanche Grant was not the only writer-historian to be fooled by such claims.

Further, in her book's frontispiece, Carson is shown standing, with his hand resting on the shoulder of the supposed explorer and soldier John C. Frémont, popularly known as the Pathfinder. That identification was long accepted as accurate. But recent scholarly investigation has demonstrated that, in reality, the man behind the beard is an obscure Edwin Perrin, rather than the famous Frémont.

Perrin had been appointed as a special agent by the War Department in Washington to see to the delivery of military supplies to Colonel Kit Carson, who then commanded New Mexico's First Volunteer Regiment on active duty in the Civil War. The picture was probably taken at Albuquerque where the Regiment was stationed during January 1862.

One other small correction requires comment. On the title page of this book, Grant states that the autobiography was dictated by Carson "to Col. and Mrs. D.C. Peters." Peters was an army surgeon and friend of Kit's. In a letter of his, printed on Grant's page 136, the doctor, indeed, makes the assertion that Carson "even dictated his life to me."

Notwithstanding, author Harvey Carter in his book *"Dear Old Kit,"* by examining the handwriting of the original manuscript and comparing it to that of the Peters couple, along with others, made a strong case that Kit's clerk at the Taos Indian agency in 1856, John Mostin, was the actual scribe. Mostin's handwriting preserved in personal letters, matches that in the Carson manuscript.

In the Sunstone reprint, essentially a facsimile of the 1926 edition, no attempt has been made to update or correct the notes supplied by Grant. Surprisingly, after so long a time, they remain useful and for the most part accurate.

Blanche C. Grant is owed credit for bringing out the first full non-embellished printing of Kit Carson's extraordinary memoir.

Blanch Chloe Grant (1874–1948) was born in Leavenworth, Kansas in 1874, daughter of Willard Webster Grant (Harvard A.B. 1869) and Mercy Ann Parsons Grant. She was a graduate of Vassar College (1896), and studied art at the Boston Museum School of Fine Arts, the Pennsylvania Academy, and at The Art League in New York. She became an established magazine illustrator and landscape painter in Wilmington, Delaware, and in 1920 moved to Taos, New Mexico and became an author and editor of books on Taos and other areas of the Southwest. Some of her other many books were: *One Hundred Years Ago in Old Taos*, *Taos Today* and *Taos Indians*. She also painted Native Americans extensively until her death in June of 1948.

III

FACSIMILE OF 1926 EDITION

Kit Carson (Standing) with His Friend John C. Fremont
Courtesy of Col. R. E. Twitchell

Kit Carson's Own Story of His Life

As dictated to Col. and Mrs. D. C. Peters
about 1856-57, and never
before published

Edited by
Blanche C. Grant

Taos, New Mexico
1926

Drawn by Kenneth M. Chapman.
This Indian design signifies wind
and rain.

The Illustration on the Cover Portrays Kit Carson
Meeting General John C. Fremont at Fort St. Vrain
on July 4, 1843. (Page 56.) Original Drawing by
Ila McAfee, Taos, New Mexico

LIST OF ILLUSTRATIONS

THE STORY OF THE MANUSCRIPT

Colonel Dewitt C. Peters, Surgeon U. S. A., was a close friend and admirer of Kit Carson, the great Taos Scout. He finally induced him to dictate his life story. This was written down, according to a son, Clinton Peters, during Carson's frequent visits to the Peters family who were stationed at "some fort near Taos", probably Fort Union and in the town of Taos as. well. In all probability, most of it was written down in the old adobe house in Taos, now owned by the Masons and called the "Kit Carson House," on the street leading eastward from the Plaza toward the mountains.

The original manuscript is for the most part in the handwriting of Mrs. Peters though at times the Colonel helped with the writing, probably in the year 1857. Col. Peters then wrote his long "Life and Adventures of Kit Carson," which was published in 1858. Carson never read the book as a whole but read enough so he is said to have remarked that Peters "laid it on a leetle too thick."

This early manuscript was evidently prized by the poet son, Theodore Peters, who took it to Paris, France. Here after his death, about 1907, his brother Clinton found the papers among his brother's effects, while rummaging around in a cellar on Ave. St. Ouen, Montmarte. Clinton Peters brought the manuscript back to New York and had two copies made. The original he sold to Edward E. Ayer for his famous Newberry Library in Chicago, Ill. The copies came into the hands of Charles L. Camp of Berkeley, California, as well as the permission from Clinton Peters, himself, to publish the story. This in turn passed to the writer.

Mr. Camp carefully compared the copy with the original and states that the story as now given is accurate except for the matter of punctuation. He has corrected certain dates for while Carson was never in error in regard to facts he did not always remember the exact year. For valuable suggestions for editorial notes the writer is indebted to Mr. Camp and also to Francis T. Cheetham of Taos, who generously gave the use of his notable collection of Carsoniana.

So save for a word inserted in parenthesis to make the meaning clear and the division into paragraphs as well as into three parts, the story is given as Carson told it, now interesting and now perhaps a bit slow but all intensely human.

It must be remembered that much of the diction of the story is undoubtedly often that of Mrs. Peters for Carson was not versed in correct English. At times, it is evident she took down his very words. Part of the manuscript has been used in articles on California written by Mr. Camp. It is now presented for the first time *as a whole* and reflects, without doubt, more truly than anything now in print, the real Carson.

Kit Carson's Own Story of His Life

PART I

1809—1842

I was born on the 24 Decr. 1809 in Madison County, Kentucky. My parents moved to Missouri when I was one year old. They settled in what is now Howard County. For two or three years after our arrival we had to remain forted and it was necessary to have men stationed at the extremities of the fields for the protection of those that were laboring.

For fifteen years I remained in Missouri. During that time I remained in Howard County. I was apprenticed[1] to David Workman to learn the saddler's trade. I remained with him two years. The business did not suit me and, having heard so many tales of life in the mountains of the West, I concluded to leave him. He was a good man, and I often recall to my mind the kind treatment I received from his hands, but taking into consideration that if I remained with him and served my apprenticeship, I would have to pass my life in labor that was distasteful to me and, being anxious to travel for the purpose of seeing different countries, I concluded to join the first party for the Rocky Mountains.

---

1. Carson's father was Lindsey Carson who seems to have wanted his son to be a lawyer but premature death under a falling log in the forest put an end to such plans. It was probably shortly after this sad event that Kit found his way to the saddler's bench.

In August, 1826, I had the fortune to hear of a party bound for that country. I made application to join this party, and, without any difficulty, I was permitted to join them.[2]

On the road, one of the party, Andrew Broadus met with a serious accident. He was taking his rifle out of a wagon for the purpose of shooting a wolf and, in drawing it out, (it) was accidently discharged, receiving the contents in the right arm. He suffered greatly from the effects of the wound. We had no medical man in the party. His arm began to mortify and we all were aware that amputation was necessary. One[3] of the party stated that he could do it. The man was prepared for any experiment to be tried that was considered of service to him. The doctor set to work and cut the flesh with a razor and sawed the bone with an old saw. The arteries being cut, to stop the bleeding, he heated a king bolt of one of the wagons and burned the affected parts, and then applied a plaster of the tar taken off the wheels of a wagon. The man became perfectly well before our arrival in New Mexico.

We arrived in Santa Fe in November, and I proceeded to Fernandez de Taos, my present place of residence, the same month, and remained during the winter with an old mountaineer by the name of Kincade.[4]

2. Carson really ran away. David Workman advertised for the runaway apprentice offering one cent for his return. "Missouri Intelligencer" issue of Oct. 12, 1826. This notice was discovered by Schwitzler a newspaper man in St. Louis, Mo.
3. Carson himself. He was only seventeen years old at the time. Peter's "Life and Adventures of Kit Carson." Page 22-24.
4. E. L. Sabin believes this man Kincade to have been a member of the family by that name in Howard County, Mo. He may have been a friend of the Carson family.

In the spring (1827) I started for the States, but, on the Arkansas River I met a party enroute for New Mexico and I joined them and remained with them till their arrival in Santa Fe. I then hired with a man (his name I have forgotten) to drive team, my wages being one dollar per day. I remained in his employ till our arrival in El Paso. I took my discharge and returned to Santa Fe.

I left Santa Fe for Taos shortly after my arrival from El Paso, and got employment of Mr. Ewing Young,[5] to do his cooking, my board being the remuneration. In the spring, (1828) I once more departed for the States, but met a party on the Arkansas, and again returned to Santa Fe. I then was employed by Col. Tramell, a merchant, as Interpreter. I accompanied him to Chihuahua and then hired with Robert McKnight[6] to go to the copper mines near the Rio Gila. I remained at the mines a few months driving team. I was not satisfied with this employment, took my discharge and departed for Taos, and arrived in August, 1828.

Some time before my arrival, Mr. Ewing Young had sent a party of trappers to the Colorado of the West.[7] They, in a fight with the Indians, were defeated, having fought all one day, and gaining no ad-

---

5. Ewing Young, who came from Knox County, Tenn., lived in Taos for at least eight years. He was a man of strong personality and always a leader. Many trapping parties were arranged by him. He finally went to California and to Oregon, probably in 1834 with Hall Kelly, where he lived the rest of his life.
6. Robert McKnight was one of a party who left Franklin, Mo. in 1812 to follow or make trails to the southwest. They reached Santa Fe and went into Mexico where they were imprisoned for ten years. He returned to Missouri but subsequently went again to Mexico where he lived for years.
7. Now called just the Colorado. At that time there were several streams known as the Colorado. Even today the Canadian River in New Mexico is called the Rio Colorado.

vantage, they considered it prudent to return. Young then raised a party of forty men, consisting of Americans, Canadians and Frenchmen, and took command himself. I joined the party which left Taos in August 1829.

In those days licenses were not granted to citizens of the United States to trap within the limits of the Mexican territory. To avoid all mistrust on the part of the Government officers, we traveled in a northern direction for fifty miles, and then changed our course to southwest, travelled through the country occupied by the Navajo Indians, passed the village of Zuni, and on to the head of the Salt River, one of the tributaries of the Rio Gila.

We, on the head waters of the Salt River, met the same Indians that had defeated the former party. Young directed the greater part of his men to hide themselves, which was done, the men concealing themselves under blankets, pack saddles, and as best they could. The hills were covered with Indians, and, seeing so few, they came to the conclusion to make an attack and drive us from our position. Our commander allowed them to enter the camp and then directed the party to fire on them, which was done, the Indians losing in killed fifteen or twenty warriors and a great number wounded. The Indians were routed, and we continued our march and trapped down the Salt River to the mouth of San Francisco river, and then up to the head of the latter stream. We were nightly harrassed by the Indians. They would frequently of nights crawl into our camp, steal a trap or so, kill a mule or horse and endeavor to do what damage they could.

The party was divided on the head of San Francisco River; one section to proceed to the valley of Sacramento in California, of which I was a member, and the other party to return to Taos for the purpose of procuring traps to replace those stolen, and to dispose of the beaver we had caught. Young took charge of the party for California consisting of eighteen men.[9]

We remained a few days after the departure of the party for Taos, for the purpose of procuring meat and making the necessary arrangement for a trip over a country never explored. Game was very scarce. After remaining three days continually on the hunt to procure the necessaries we had only killed three bears, the skins of which we took off in such a manner as to make tanks for the purpose of carrying water. We then started on our expedition in the best of spirits, having heard from the Indians that the streams of the valley to which we were going were full of beaver, but that the country over which we were to travel was very barren, and that we would suffer very much for want of water; the truth of which we very soon knew.

The first four days march was over a country, sandy, burned up and not a drop of water. We received at night a small quantity of water from the tanks which we had been fortunate to have along. A

---

9.   See account of this expedition as told by George Nidever in Bancroft Library, Berkeley.

guard was placed over the tanks to prohibit anyone from making use of more than his due allowance.

After four days travel we found water. Before we reached the water the pack mules were strung along the road for several miles. They having smelt the water long before we had any hopes of finding any, and then each animal made the best use of the strength left them after their severe sufferings to reach the water as soon as they could. We remained two days. It would have been impracticable to have continued the march without giving the men and animals rest they so much required.

After remaining encamped (two) days we started on our expedition and for four days travelled over a country similar to that which we travelled over before our arrival to the last water. There was not any water to be found during this time, and we suffered extremely on account of it. On the fourth day we arrived on the Colorado of the West, below the great Cañon. It can better be imagined, our joy, than described when we discovered the stream.

We had suffered greatly for want of food. We met a party of the Mohave Indians and purchased of them a mare, heavy with foal. The mare was killed and eaten by the party with great gusto; even the foal was devoured. We encamped on the banks of the Colorado three days, recruiting our animals and trading for provisions with the Indians. We procured of them a few beans and corn. Then we took a southwestern course and in three days march, struck the bed of a stream which rises in the coast range, has a northeast course, and is lost in the sands of the Great Basin. We proceeded up the stream[10] for six days. In two days after our arrival on the stream we found water. We then left the stream and travelled in a westerly direction and in four days, arrived at the Mission of San Gabriel.

At the Mission there was one priest, fifteen soldiers, and about one thousand Indians. They had about eighty thousand head of stock, fine fields and vineyards, in fact, it was paradise on earth. We remained one day at the Mission, received good treatment of the inhabitants, and purchased of them what beef we required. We had nothing but butcher knives to trade, and for four they would give us a beef. We received information from the Missionaries of the Mission of San Fernando, we travelled for the Mission, found pass through the mountain.

In one day's travel from this Mission, we reached the mission of San Fernando having about the same number of inhabitants, but not carried on as large as the one of San Gabriel. We then took a northwest course and passed the mountains to the valley of the Sacremento. We had plenty to eat and found grass in abundance for our animals. We found signs of trappers on the San Joaquin. We followed their trail and, in a few days, overtook the party and found them to be of the Hudson Bay Company. They were sixty men strong, commanded by Peter Ogden. We trapped down the San Joaquin and its tributaries and found but little beaver, but game plenty,

10. This stream was undoubtedly the river now called the Mojave in California.

elk, deer, and antelope in thousands. We travelled near each other until we came to the Sacramento; then we separated, Ogden taking up the Sacramento for Columbia river. We remained during the summer. Not being the season for trapping, we passed our time in hunting.

During our stay on the Sacramento a party of Indians of the Mission of San Rafael (San José) ran away and took refuge at a village of Indians who were not friendly with those of the Mission. The priest of San Rafael sent a party of fifteen Indians in pursuit. They applied for assistance from a village that was friendly and were furnished with the number they required. They then moved towards the village where the runaways were concealed and demanded them to be given up, which was refused. They attacked the village and after a severe struggle they were compelled to retreat. They came to us and requested assistance. Mr. Young directed me and eleven men to join. We turned to the village and made an attack, fought for one entire day. The Indians were routed, lost a great number of men. We entered the village in triumph, set fire to it and burned it to the ground.

The next day we demanded the runaways and informed them that if not immediately given up we would not leave one of them alive. They complied with our demands. We turned over our Indians to those from whom they had deserted and we returned to our camp.

Miss Blanche C. Grant and Her Friends, Colonel Dick Rutledge
and Francis T. Cheetham

Mr. Young and four of us proceeded with the Indians to San Rafael. We took with us the beaver we had on hand. We were well received by the missionaries.

At the Mission we found a trading schooner, the Captain of which was ashore. We traded with him our furs and for the money, purchased horses of those at the Mission, and having purchased all we required returned to our camp. Shortly afterwards a party of Indians during the night came to our camp, frightened our animals and ran off some sixty head. Fourteen were discovered in the morning. Twelve of us saddled and took the trail of the lost animals, pursued them upwards of one hundred miles into the Sierra Nevada. We surprised the Indians when feasting of(f) some of our animals they had killed. We charged their camp, killed eight Indians, took three children prisoners and recovered all our animals with the exception of six that were eaten and returned to our camp.

On the first September we struck camp and returning by the same route which we had come, passing through San Fernando. We traveled to the Pueblo of Los Angeles, where the Mexican authorities demanded our passports. We had none. They wished to arrest us, but fear deterred them. They then commenced selling liquor to the men, no doubt for the purpose of getting the men drunk so that they would have but little difficulty in making the arrest. Mr. Young discovered their intention, directed me to take three men, all loose animals, packs, etc. and go in advance. He would remain with the balance of the party and endeavor to get them along. If he did not arrive at my camp by next morning I was directed to move on as best I could and, on my return to report the party killed; for Young would not leave them. They were followed by the Mexicans, furnishing them all the liquor they could pay for. All got drunk except Young.

The Mexicans would have continued with them till they arrived at the Mission of San Gabriel, then, being re-inforced, arrest the party, only for a man by the name of James Higgins dismounting from his horse and deliberately shooting James Lawrence. Such conduct frightened the Mexicans, and they departed in all haste, fearing that, if men, without provocation, would shoot one another, it would require but little to cause them to murder them.

About dark Young and party found me. The next day we departed and pursued nearly the same route by which we came, and in nine days we arrived on the Colorado. Two days after our arrival, on the Colorado, at least five hundred Indian warriors came to our camp. They pretended friendship, but such a large number coming, we mistrusted them, and closely watched their maneouvers. We discovered where they had their weapons concealed, and then it became apparent to us that their design was to murder the party. There were but few of us in camp, the greater number being out visiting the traps. I considered the safest way to act was not to let the Indians know of our mistrust and to act in a fearless manner. One of the Indians could speak Spanish. I directed him to state to the Indians that they must leave our camp inside of ten minutes. If one should be found after the expiration of that time, he would be shot. Before the expiration of the ten minutes, everyone had left.

We trapped down the south side of Colorado river to tide water without any further molestation, and up the north side to the mouth of San Pedro. Near the mouth of the San Pedro we saw a large herd of animals, horses, etc. We knew that Indians were near and, not having forgot the damage those same Indians done, we concluded to deprive them of their stock. We charged their camp. They fled, and we took possession of the animals.

The same evening we heard a noise, something like the sound of distant thunder. We sprung for our arms and sallied out to reconnoiter. We discovered a party of Indians driving some two hundred horses. We charged them, firing a few shots. The Indians run, leaving us the sole possessors of the horses. Those horses had been stolen by the Indians from Mexicans in Sonora.

Having now more animals than we could take care of, we concluded to dispose of them to best advantage. We chose out as many as we required for riding and packing purposes, killed ten, dried the meat to take with us and let the balance loose, I presume the Indians got them.

We continued up the Gila to opposite the copper mines. We went to the mines, found Robert Mc-Knight and there left our beaver with him. We could not bring it to the settlements to dispose of on account of not having license to trap in Mexican territory. We concealed our beaver in one of the deep holes dug by the miners. Young and I remained a few days at the mines, the balance of the party had started for Taos. Young and I went to Santa Fe. He procured a license to trade with Indians on the Gila. He sent a few men to the mines to get the beaver he had concealed. They got it and returned to Santa Fe. Every one considered we had made a fine trade in so short a period. They were not aware that we had been months trapping. The Beaver was disposed of to advantage at Santa Fe, some two thousand pounds in all.

In April 1830 (1831 probably) we had all safely arrived at Taos. The amount due us was paid, and each of us having several hundred dollars, we passed the time gloriously, spending our money freely never thinking that our lives were risked in gaining it. Our only idea was to get rid of the dross as soon as possible but at the same time, have as much pleasure and enjoyment as the country could afford. Trappers and sailors are similar in regard to the money that they earn so dearly, daily being in danger of losing their lives. But when the voyage has been made (and they have) received their pay, they think not of the hardships and danger through which they have passed, spend all they have and are ready for another trip. In all probability, (they) have to be furnished with all that is necessary for their outfit.

In the fall of 1830 (1831) I joined the party

under Fitzpatrick[11] for the Rocky Mountains on a trapping expedition.[12] We traveled north till we struck the Platte river and then took up the Sweet Water, a branch of the Platte. We trapped to the head of the Sweet Water and then on to Green River, and then on to Jackson's Hole, a fork of the Columbia River; and from there on to the head of Salmon River. Then we came to the camp of a part of our band that we had been hunting, then we went into winter quarters on the head of Salmon River. During winter we lost some four or five men when out hunting Buffalo. They have been killed by the Blackfeet Indians.

In April 1831, (1832) we commenced our hunt again. We trapped back to the Bear River, the principal stream that empties into the Great Salt Lake, then on to the Green River. We then found a party of trappers under charge of Mr. Sinclair. They left Taos shortly after we had. They had wintered on little Bear River, a branch of Green. They told me that Captain Gaunt[13] was in the New Park, that he and party had wintered near the Laramie. I wished to join his party. Four of us left the party and struck out in search of Gaunt. In ten days, we found him and party at the New Park.

We remained trapping in the Park for some

11. Thomas Fitzpatrick was a noted leader of trapping parties during the early part of the century. He is often mentioned by writers of that day.
12. H. R. Tilton, ass't. surgeon U. S. Army, wrote of Carson under the date of January 7th, 1874, "As I was a successful amateur trapper, he threw off all reserve, and greeted me with more than usual warmth, saying, 'the happiest days of my life were spent in trapping.' " J. S. C. Abbott, "Kit Carson" Pg. 343.
13. Captain Gaunt or Gant or Grant. All three names are used by various authorities.

time, and then through the plains of Laramie and on
to the south fork of the Platte, then to the Arkansas.
On our arrival on the Arkansas, Gaunt took the beaver we had caught to Taos. The party remained on
the Arkansas trapping. The beaver was disposed
of, the necessaries for our camp were purchased and,
in the course of two months, Gaunt joined (us). We
trapped on the waters of the Arkansas until the river
began to freeze, and then went into winter quarters
on the main stream. During the winter we passed
a pleasant time. The snow was very deep and we had
no difficulty in procuring as much buffalo meat as
we required.

In January (1833) a party of men had been out
hunting and returned about dark. Their horses were
very poor, having been fed during the winter on
cottonwood bark; they turned them out to gather
such nourishment as they could. That night a party
of about fifty Crow Indians came to our camp and
stole nine of the horses that were loose. In the morning we discovered sign of the Indians and twelve of
us took the trail of the Indians and horses. We traveled some forty miles. It was getting late. Our animals were fatigued for the course over which we
came (was difficult) The snow was deep, and many
herds of buffaloes having passed during the day,
was the cause of our having a great deal of difficulty, keeping the trail.

We saw, at a distance of two or three miles, a
grove of timber. Taking into consideration the condition of our animals, we concluded to make for the

timber and camp for the night. On our arrival, we
saw fires some four miles ahead of us. We tied our
animals to trees, and as soon as it became dark, took
a circuitous route for the Indian Camp.

We were to come on the Indians from the direction in which they were traveling. It took us some
time to get close enough to the camp to discover
their strength, as we had to crawl, and used all means
that we were aware of, to elude detection. After considerable crawling, etc. we came within about one
hundred yards of their camp. The Indians were in
two forts of about equal strength. They were danc-
ing and singing, and passing the night jovially in
honor of the robbery committed by them on the
whites. We saw our horses, they were tied at the
entrance of the fort. Let come what would we were
bound to get our horses. We remained concealed in
the brush until they laid down to sleep, suffering
from the cold.

When we thought they were all asleep, six of us
crawled towards the animals. (The) remainder was
to remain where they were as a reserve for us to fall
back on in case of not meeting with success. By hiding behind logs and crawling silently towards the
fort, the snow being of great service to us for when
crawling we were not liable to make any noise.

We finally reached the horses, cut the ropes, and
by throwing snow balls at them drove them to where
was stationed our reserve. We then held council
taking the views of each in regard to what had best
be done. Some were in favor of retiring; having recovered their property and received no damage, they

would be willing to return to camp. Not so with those that had lost no animals. They wanted satisfaction for the trouble and hardships they had gone through while in pursuit of the thieves. Myself and two more were the ones that had not lost horses and we were determined to have satisfaction, let the consequences be ever so fatal. The peace party could not get a convert to their side. Seeing us so determined to fight (there is always a brotherly affection existing among the trappers and the side of danger always being their choice) we were not long before all agreed to join us in our perilous enterprise.

We started the horses that were retaken to the place where we tied our other animals, with three men as escort.

We then marched direct for the fort from which we got our horses. When within a few paces of the fort, a dog discovered us and commenced barking. The Indians were alarmed and commenced getting up. We opened a deadly fire, each ball taking its victim. We killed nearly every Indian in the fort. The few that remained were wounded and made their escape to the other fort, the Indians of which commenced firing on us; but without any effect, we, keeping concealed behind trees and only firing when we were sure of our object. It was now near day, the Indians could see our forces, as it being so weak, they concluded to charge on us. We received them and when very close, fired on them, killing five and the balance returned to their fort. After some deliberation among the Indians, they finally made another attempt which met with greater success to them. We

Kit Carson, the Soldier
Colonel, U.S. Army

had to retreat. But there being much timber in the vicinity, we had but little difficulty in making our camp, and then, being reinforced by the three men with the horses, we awaited the approach of the enemy. They did not attack us. We started for our main camp and arrived in the evening.[14]

---

14. George Bird Grinnell in his article, "Bent's Old Fort and its Builders" Kan. Hist. So. Pub. Vol. XV retells Black Whitman's version of this fight. It seems that all the animals but two had been stolen and that meant Carson's party must regain their property or wait many weary days for more to be brought from New Mexico. The Crows had gone north with the horses and made camp where they believed Carson and his small party of eleven would hardly dare to come since they were sixty strong. Grinnell says, "Twilight was falling when Carson's party, the two mounted Cheyennes still out ahead, following the trail in the snow across the prairie, saw a shower of sparks rising from a thicket some distance in front of them. The party halted and held another consultation. Black Whiteman and Little Turtle then rode off alone while Carson drew up his men in a long line, each man several paces from his neighbors on either side.

As they advanced swiftly across the snow a dog barked in the thicket, and a moment later a little ball of white steam shot up from the willows. The Crows had put out their fire with snow. The Americans quickened their pace and had almost reached the edge of the thicket when without warning sixty Crow warriors broke out of the willows and charged them. So fierce and sudden was the attack that Carson and his men were borne back and almost surrounded; then they drew up their rifles and gave the Indians a volley.

Carson used to tell how surprised the Crows were when they charged in on his little party and were met by this stunning volley. Back into the thicket went the Crows and in after them went Carson and his men. The Indians evidently intended to mount and either run away or continue to fight on horseback, but when they reached their camp in the middle of the thicket they found that the horses and mules they had left there had disappeared. Right at their heels came Carson's men; so without halting the Indians rushed on through the thicket and out at the far side, making across the prairie as fast as they could go. The whites, worn out after long march through the snow and content with the result of the fight, did not attempt to follow farther.

When Carson had started to advance toward the willows, Black Whiteman and Little Turtle had ridden off to one side, making toward one end of the thicket; then just as the Crows charged out of the bushes the two Cheyennes rode in, stampeded the horses and mules and ran them down the creek. They went a mile or two and then left the herd in the timber and hurried back to join the fight; but when they reached the thicket they found Carson and his men resting in the Crow camp, the fight having ended as quickly as it had begun. It was dark by this time, and after resting for awhile the two Cheyennes led the whole party down to the place where they had left the horses and mules. Here a big fire was built in the timber and the tired men lay down on the snow.

In the morning Black Whiteman and Little Turtle returned to the thicket, and there found, counted coup on, and scalped two dead Crows.

The Cheyennes have always expressed surprise that in this fight Carson and his men, all well armed and excellent shots, should have killed only two Crows. What was not less surprising was that although in their first rush the Crows came almost to

During our pursuit for the lost animals we suffered considerably but, in the success of having recovered our horses, and sending many a red skin to
his long home, our sufferings were soon forgotten.
We remained in our camp without any further molestation until Spring (1833). We then started for Laramie on another trapping expedition.

Before our departure we cached what beaver
we had on hand, some four hundred pounds. When
we arrived on the south fork of the Platte, two men
of the party deserted, taking with them three of our
best animals. We suspected their design, and Gaunt
sent myself and another man in pursuit. They had
a day the start and we could not overtake them.
When we arrived at our old camp, we discovered that
they had raised the beaver and taken (it) down the
Arkansas in a canoe which we had made during the
winter for the purpose of crossing the river. The
men and beaver we never heard of. I presume they
were killed by Indians. Such a fate they should receive for their dishonesty. The animals we recovered
and considered ourselves happy; they being of much
more service to us than men that we could never
more trust.

We took possession of one of the buildings that
were built during the winter and made the necessary
preparations for our defense—not having the re-
motest idea how long we should have to remain. Being by ourselves we never ventured very far from

---

hand-to-hand fighting with Carson's men, not one of the whites
was killed or received a serious wound." Such is Black Whiteman's story as he counted coups, a ceremony among Indians when
every Indian is pledged to the truth."

our fort, unless for the purpose of procuring meat. We kept our horses picketed near and, at night, slept in the house, always keeping a good lookout so that we might not be surprised when unprepared. We remained about a month and Mr. Blackwell, Gaunt's partner, arrived from the States. He had with him some ten or fifteen men. Shortly after their arrival four trappers of Gaunt's party arrived. They were sent to find us to see whether we were dead or alive, the former being the general belief.

We remained only a few days after the arrival of the trappers. They stated that Gaunt's camp was in the Ballo Salado (Bayou Salado) the head waters of the south head of the Platte.

When four days on the march, we were all sitting eating of our breakfast, we discovered a party of Indians trying to steal our horses. We suspected no danger and had turned our horses out to graze,—some hobbled and some loose. As soon as we perceived the Indians we made for them. They run off. One Indian was killed. They only stole from us one horse; one of the Indians having been lucky enough to have mounted one of the loose horses and made his escape.

We then traveled that day about fifty miles and thought that we had got clear of the Indians. We camped on a beautiful stream, one of the tributaries of the Arkansas.

During the night we had our best animals staked. We had with us a very watchful dog and during the night he kept continually barking. We were aware of the Indians being close and kept good watch. In the morning myself, and three others, proposed going to a fork that we knew of. It was not far, and we wished to visit (it) to see for Beaver sign. If good we intended to trap it; if not, to proceed on our journey.

About an hour after we left, a large party of Indians charged the camp running off all the loose animals. Four men immediately mounted four of the best animals and followed and in a short time overtook the Indians and recaptured all of the animals. One of the four was severely wounded in the affray. One Indian was killed.

The route which we had to go to reach the fork was over a mountain that was difficult to pass. After some trouble, we crossed and arrived at our destination, but found no beaver sign. On our return we took a different route from that which we had come.

As we got around the mountain and were near our former trail, I saw in the distance, four Indians. I proposed to charge them. All were willing. We started for them, but, when near we found we had caught a tartar. There were upward of sixty Indians. They had surrounded us and our only chance to save our lives was a good run. We done so,[15] the Indians firing on us from all directions. We run the guantlet for about two hundred yards, the Indians were often as near as twenty yards of us. We durst not fire, not knowing what moment our horses

---

15. Carson, it must be remembered, had little or no schooling. He never read much and did not learn to write, it is said, until he was an officer in the Civil War.

might be shot from under us and the idea of being
left afoot, your gun unloaded, was enough for to
make any man retain the shot which his gun con-
tained. We finally made our escape and joined the
party at the camp. One of the men was severely
wounded, it being the only damage we received.

On our arrival at camp we were informed of
what had transpired during our absence. It was
then easy enough to account for the Indians having
followed us. They saw us leave camp and, as they
had the misfortune to lose the animals they had stol-
en, they intended to have our scalps. They made a
very good attempt, but, thank God! failed.

We made a fort and remained encamped for the
night—could not move until the wounded men were
properly cared for. In the morning we made a litter
to carry one of the wounded (the other could ride
horseback) and then pursued our course and in four
days march we found Gaunt, remained at his camp
until our wounded men recovered, then started for
the Old Park. We found beaver scarce, there having
been so many trappers before us.

I, and two others, concluded to leave the party
and go make a hunt on our own hook. We trapped
nearly all the streams within the mountains, keeping
from the plains from fear of danger. We had very
good luck, having caught a great amount of beaver,
we started for Taos to dispose of it and then have the
pleasure of spending the money that caused us so
much danger and hardship to earn.

We arrived at Taos in October, 1832 (1833), disposed of (our) beaver for a good sum, and everything of mountain life was forgotten for the time present.

In Taos, I found Captain Lee[16] of the U. S. A., a partner of Bent and St. Vrain. He purchased goods to trade with the trappers. I joined him and in the latter part of the month of October we started for the mountains to find the trappers.

We followed the Spanish trail that leads to California till we struck White River, took down the White River till we struck Green River, crossed Green to the Wintey (Unitah) one of its tributaries. There we found Mr. Robidoux.[17] He had a party of some twenty men that were trapping and trading.

The snow was now commencing to fall and we concluded to go into winter quarters. We found a place that answered every purpose on the mouth of the Wintey. We passed a very pleasant winter and in March we heard of Mr. Fitzpatrick[18] and Bridger being on Snake River. During the winter a California Indian of Mr. Robidoux party run off with six animals,—some of them being worth two hundred dollars per head. Robidoux came to me and requested that I should pursue him. I spoke to Captain Lee and he informed me that I might use my pleasure. There was a Utah village close by, I got one

16. Capt. Stephen Luis Lee was well known in Taos and killed in the Taos uprising in 1847.
17. This was probably Antoine Robidoux a brother to the men who founded St. Joseph, Mo., and Riverside, California. He was very early in the mountains.
18. Fitzpatrick was well known as "Major" Fitzpatrick in the trapping country, about whose character there seems to have been a difference of opinion among the early mountain men. Bridger, on the other hand, seems to have enjoyed the respect of all and was probably an even greater mountain man than Carson. He claimed to have taught Carson what he knew of mountain ways.

of the Indians to accompany me. We were furnished with two fine animals and took the trail (of) the runaway had taken down the river, his object being to make California.

When travelling about one hundred miles the animal of the Indian gave out. He would not accompany me any further, but I was determined not to give up the chase. I continued in pursuit and in thirty miles I overtook the Indian with the horses. Seeing me by myself, (he) showed fight. I was under the necessity of killing him, recovered the horses, and returned on my way to our camp, and arrived in a few days without any trouble.

Some trappers came to our camp and informed us that Fitzpatrick and Bridger were on the Snake River encamped. In March, (1834) we struck out for the purpose of finding their camp. In fifteen days, we found their camp. Then Captain Lee sold his goods to Fitzpatrick to be paid in beaver. When paid, Lee started for Taos. I joined Fitzpatrick and remained with him one month. He had a great many men in his employ, and I thought it best to get three men and go hunt by our selves. I done so. We passed the summer trapping on the head of Laramie and its tributaries, keeping to the mountains, our party being too weak to venture on the plains.

One evening, when we were on the route to join Bridger's party after I had selected the camp for the night, I gave my horse to one of the men and started on foot for the purpose of killing something for supper, not having a particle of anything eatable on

hand. I had gone about a mile and discovered some
elk. I was on the side of a ridge. I shot one and
immediately after the discharge of my gun, I heard
in my rear a noise. I turned around and saw two
very large grizzly bears making for me. My gun
was unloaded and I could not possibly reload it in
time to fire. There were some trees at a short distance. I made for them, the bears after me. As I
got to one of the trees, I had to drop my gun, the
bears rushing for me I had to make all haste to ascend the tree. I got up some ten or fifteen feet and
then had to remain till the bears would find it convenient to leave. One remained but a short time, the
other remained for some time and with his paws
would nearly unroot the small aspen trees that were
around the one which I had ascended. He made several attempts at the one in which I was, but could
do no damage. He finally concluded to leave, of
which I was heartily pleased, never having been so
scared in my life.[19] I remained in the tree for some
time, and, when I considered the bears far enough
off, I descended and made for my camp in as great
haste as possible. It was dark when I arrived and
(I) could not send for the elk which I had killed,
so we had to pass the night without anything to eat.
During the night we caught beaver, so we had something for breakfast.

We remained in this place (head of the Laramie) some ten or fifteen days when Bridger came
making his way for summer rende(z)vous (1834).
We joined him and went to Green River (the place

19. Carson is said to have called this experience his "worst difficult."

of rendezvous). Here was two camps of us. I think
that there was two hundred trappers encamped.
Then, till our supplies came from St. Louis, we disposed of our beaver to procure supplies. Coffee and
sugar were two dollars a pint, powder the same, lead
one dollar a bar and common blankets from fifteen
to twenty five dollars apiece.

We remained in rende(z)vous during August
(1834) and in September camp was broken up and
we divided into parties of convenient size and started on our fall hunt. In the party of which I was a
member then, (there) were fifty men.

We set out for the country of the Blackfeet Indians, on the head waters of the Missouri. We made
a very poor hunt as the Indians were very bad. Five
of our men were killed. A trapper could hardly go
a mile without being fired upon. As we found that
we could do but little in their country, so we started
for winter quarters.

In November (1834) we got to Big Snake River,
where we camped. We remained here till February.
1833 (1835). Nothing of moment having transpired
till February, (when) the Blackfeet came and stole
eighteen horses. Twelve of us followed them and
caught up in about fifty miles. They had travelled
as far as they could on account of the snow. We endeavored to get the horses (some shots had been
fired) but could not approach near enough to the Indians to do any damage. They had snow shoes, we
had none, they could travel over the snow without
any difficulty, we would sink in the snow to our
waists.

The horses were on the side of a hill where there was but little snow. Our only object now was to get the horses. We wished a parley. The Indians agreed. One man from each (side) was to proceed halfway the distance between us and have a talk.

It was done. We talked some; the Indians saying that they thought we were Snake Indians (and that they) did not wish to steal from the Whites. We informed them that if they were friendly why did they not lay down their arms and have a friendly talk and smoke. They agreed and laid down their arms. We done the same. One man to guard the arms. We then met at the place where the two first were talking (and) talked and smoked.

The Indians were thirty strong. They sent for the horses, (but) only returned with five of the worst. They said (they) would not give any more. We broke for our arms, they for theirs. Then the fight commenced. I and Markhead[20] was in the advance, approaching two Indians that were remaining in the rear concealed behind two trees. I approaching one and Markhead the other. Markhead was not paying sufficient attention to the Indian who, I noticed, him raise his gun to fire. I forgot entirely the danger in which I was myself and neglected my Indian for the one of Markhead's. As the Indian was ready to fire on Markhead, I raised my gun and took sight. The Indian saw it (and endeavored to conceal him-

---

20. Markhead was killed in the attack on Turley's mill near Taos in Jan. 1847. Ruxton.

self. I fired and he fell. The moment I fired I thought of the Indian that I was after. I noticed him. He was sighting for my breast. I could not load in time so I commenced dodging as well as I could. He fired, the ball grazed my neck and passed through my shoulder.

We then drew off for about a mile and encamped for the night. It was very cold (and we) could not make any fires for fear the Indians might approach and fire on us. We had no covering but our saddle blankets. I passed a miserable night from the pain of the wound, (it having bled freely) which was frozen.

In the morning the Indians were in the same place. We were not strong enough to attack, so we started for camp. Bridger with thirty men then started for the place where we had left the Indians, but when they arrived the Indians had gone to the plains and of the stolen animals we had only recovered the five which they had given us.

In a few days we set (out) on our spring hunt, trapped the waters of the Snake and Green Rivers, made a very good hunt and then went into Summer quarters on Green River (1835).

Shortly after making rendezvous our equipment arrived, then we disposed of our beaver to the traders that came up with our equipments. We remained in summer quarters till September.

There was in the party of Captain Drips[21] a large Frenchman,[22] one of those overbearing kind and very strong. He made a practice of whipping every man that he was displeased with,—and that was nearly all. One day, after he had beaten two or three men, he said, that for the Frenchmen he had no trouble to flog and, as for the Americans, he would take a switch and switch them.

I did not like such talk from any man, so I told him that I was the worst American in camp. Many could trash (thrash) him only (they didn't) on account of being afraid and that if he made use of any more such expressions, I would rip his guts.

He said nothing but started for his rifle, mounted his horse and made his appearance in front of the camp. As soon as I saw him, I mounted my horse and took the first arms I could get hold of, which was a pistol, galloped up to him and demanded if I was the one which he intended to shoot. Our horses (were) touching. He said no, but at the same time drawing his gun so he could have a fair shot at me.

21. Captain Drips was a noted mountain guide given however, to dogging the footsteps of successful trappers for which he was cordially disliked. He was with members of the American Fur Company and followed Bridger who was of the Rocky Mt. Fur Co.
22. Shunan or Shunar. Rev. Samuel Parker was an eye witness of this affair and wrote of it. He was a missionary enroute for Oregon.
    "I will relate an occurrence which took place near evening as a specimen of mountain life. A hunter who goes techniquely by the name of the great bully of the mountains mounted his horse with a loaded rifle and challenged any Frenchman, American, Spaniard or Dutchman to fight him in single combat. Kit Carson, an American, told him if he wished to die, he would accept the challenge. Shunar (also written Shunan) defied him. Carson mounted his horse and with a loaded pistol rushed into close contact and both almost at the same instant fired. C's ball entered S's hand came out at the wrist and passed through the arm above the elbow. S's ball passed over the head of C. and while he went for another pistol Shunar begged that his life be spared. Such scenes, sometimes from passion and sometimes for amusement, make the pastime of their wild and wandering life."

I was prepared and allowed him to draw his gun. We both fired at the same time; all present saying that but one report was heard. I shot him through the arm and his ball passed my head, cutting my hair and the powder burning my eye, the muzzle of his gun being near my head when he fired. During our stay in camp we had no more bother with this bully (of a) Frenchman.

On the first (of) September, (1835) we departed on our Fall hunt, trapping the Yellow Stone, and Big Horn Rivers, and crossed over to the Three Forks of the Missouri (and up the North Fork) and wintered on Big Snake River and its tributaries. There we found Thomas McCoy, one of the Hudson Bay traders. Antoine Godey, four more and myself joined McCoy having heard of Mary's River (now called the Humboldt) and beaver on it was plenty.

Trapped down Mary's River (to) where (it) loses itself in the great basin, and found few beaver. Then we went up it some sixty miles, then struck across to the waters of Big Snake River. There we separated. McCoy going to Fort Walla Walla and we went to Fort Hall. On our march we found no game, the country was barren. For many days the only food we (had) was roots and we would bleed our horses and cook the blood.

About four days travel before we got to the fort we met a party of Indians. I traded with them for a fat horse, which we killed, feasted for a couple of days and started for the Fort where we safely arrived.

We were received kindly by the people, treated well and remained a few days, then started to hunt buffalo, they not being more than a couple of days travel from the fort. We killed a good many buffalo and returned to the Fort. The Blackfeet Indians must have seen us when hunting, for that night they came to the Fort and stole every animal we had.

We were encamped outside of the Fort, but our animals (were) in one of the corrals belonging to it. During the night the sentinel saw two men approach and let down the bars and drive out the animals, thinking that it was one of us, turning out the animals to graze. We were now afoot and had to remain. In about a month McCoy came and (we) joined him and started for the rendezvous on Green River[23] (1836). He had plenty of animals and we purchased of him.

In six days travel we reached the rendezvous at the mouth of Horse Creek on Green River, remaining in rendezvous some twenty days. McCoy went back to Fort Hall. I joined Fontenelle's party and we started for the Yellowstone. Our party was one hundred strong,—fifty trappers and fifty camp keepers. We had met with so much difficulty from the Blackfeet that this time, as we were in force, we determined to trap wherever we pleased, even if we had to fight for the right.

---

23. Green River was the scene of many a rendevous of the hunters. Its long course through what is now Wyoming and its many tributaries made it a natural place for the trappers to meet. The phrase "up to the Green River" referred not to the river but to the name cut on the handle and used as a trade name for a hunting knife.

We trapped the Yellow Stone, Otter and Muscle Shell Rivers and then up the Big Horn and on to Powder River, where we wintered. During our hunt we had no fights with the Blackfeet, we could not know the cause. Near our encampment was the Crow Indian village. They were friendly and remained together during the winter. They informed us of the reason of us not being harrassed by the Blackfeet during our hunt. It was that the small-pox[24] was among them and they had gone north of the Missouri, then none remained on our hunting ground.

We remained in camp on Powder River till the first of April (1837). We passed in camp a pleasant time. Only it was one of the coldest winters I ever experienced. For fear of danger we had to keep our animals in a corral. The feed furnished them was cottonwood bark, which we would pull from the trees and then throw it by the fire.

We had to keep the buffalo from our camp by building large fires in the bottoms. They came in such large droves that our horses were in danger of being killed when we turned them out to eat of the branches of trees which we had cut down. When (we) broke up camp and started two men for Fort Laramie where the American Fur Company had established a trading post. They never reached this. I presume they were killed by the Sioux Indians.

We then commenced our hunt trapping the streams we had in the Fall to the Yellow Stone and up Twenty Five Yard River to the three forks of the

24. Small pox was the foe of the Indians. It has been estimated that at one time about a million Indians died of this plague in the southwest.

Missouri and then up the North Fork of the Missouri. There we found that the small-pox had not killed all the Blackfeet for there was a large village of them in advance of us. We cautiously travelled on their trail till we found they were only one day ahead. Six of us then left the main party to pursue the Indians (and) to find out their strength; the balance of the party continuing its march in our rear. We discovered them. They were driving in their animals and making preparations to move their camp. We joined the main party and gave the information of the movements of the Indian village.

We had come within four miles of their village and, as we were determined to try our strength, to discover who had the right to the country, I with forty men started for the village, sixty men being left to guard the camp and we soon reached the village, attacked it and killed ten Indians. The fight commenced and we continued advancing, they retreating for about three hours. Our ammunition began to give out, the Indians were soon aware of the fact. They then knowing that they had advantage of us turned upon us. We fought them as well as we could considering the scarcity of our ammunition. We run retreating for our camp. The Indians would often charge among us. We would turn and give fire. They would retreat, then we would continue our course.

As we were passing a point of rocks the horse of Cotton fell. He was held to the ground by the weight of his horse. Six Indians made for him for the purpose of taking his scalp. I dismounted, fired and

The Carson Monument in Trinidad, Colo. and Three Old-Timers
Who Knew Carson

killed one Indian. The balance run. By this time Cotton had got released from the pressure of him, his horse had arose and he mounted and made the camp.

When I fired my horse got frightened and broke away from me and found the party in advance. I noticed White (he was not far from me), called him and, as soon as he saw the predicament I was in, he came to me. I mounted his horse (behind him) and we continued our retreat and soon reached our camp.

The Indians took position in a pile of rocks about one hundred and fifty yards from us. They commenced firing on us. We returned their fire, but, finding that no execution could be done, we concluded to charge them, done so. It was the prettiest fight I ever saw. The Indians stood for some time. I would often see a white man on one side and an Indian on the other side of a rock, not ten feet apart each dodging and trying to get the first shot.

We finally routed them and took several scalps, having several of our men slightly wounded. This ended our difficulties with the Blackfeet for the present hunt.

We continued up the north fork to the head of Green River when an express[25] overtook us, saying that the rendezvous (1837) would be on Wind River. We then started for the rendezvous, arrived in eight days. Our equipments had come up, also some missionaries for the Columbia, also an Englishman, Sir.

25. An express was one or more often two men on horseback sent on to give some definite news.

William Stuart,[26]—a man that will be forever remembered by the mountaineers that had the honor of his acquaintance, for his liberality to them and for his many good qualities.

Among the missionaries was old Father de Smitt (Smedt)[27] now at the Catholic University of St. Louis. I can say of him that if ever there was a man wished to do good he is one. He never feared danger when duty required his presence among the savages, and, if good works on this earth are rewarded hereafter, I am confident that his share of glory and happiness in the next world will be great.

In twenty days the rendezvous broke up, and I and seven men went to Brown's Hole,[28] a trading post. I there joined Thompson and Sinclair's party on a trading exposition to the Navajo Indians.

We traded for thirty miles. We returned to Brown's Hole. After our arrival Thompson took the mules to the South Fork of the Platte, disposed of them to Sublett[29] and Vasques, and returned with goods that would answer for trading with Indians. I was now employed as hunter for the Fort and continued as such during the winter. I had to keep twenty men in provisions.

---

26. "Sir William Stuart was one of several titled Englishmen who came to the Rockies for the sheer love of sport and won, as most of them did, the respect of the old-time mountain men.

27. Father de Smedt was a rover among the Indians for many years and seems to have been the most beloved by the mountain men of all the missionaries who came to serve the Indians. He was an unusual man. Carson always spoke in highest terms of Father de Smedt. Carson himself was a Protestant and a Mason.

28. The word "Hole" usually meant a small valley in the early parlance of the mountains.

29. The brothers Sublette were well and favorably known throughout the mountains. William L. Sublette and Milton Sublette seem to have been the leaders. As traders in fur they were very successful.

In the Spring, (1838), I joined Bridger. In the party there was myself, Dick Owens and three Canadians. We five started for the Black Hills to hunt. We trapped the streams in the vicinity of the hills. We separated,—Owens and myself taking one course, and the Canadians another. We trapped for three months, made a good hunt and then started to find the main camp. We found it on a tributary of Green River. We remained with the main party till July (1838) and then went into rendezvous on the Popoaghi, a tributary of Wind River. About the 20th of August, we started for Yellow Stone, trapped all the streams within the vicinity of Yellow Stone and on it went into Winter quarters.

About the first of January (1839) a few men were out hunting not far from camp, and discovered a party of Blackfeet. As soon as information was brought us of the nearness of our old enemies, a party of forty men started to meet them and we drove them on an island in the Yellow Stone, where they strongly fortified themselves. It was late when we commenced the attack. We continued the fight till Sunset, and then had to retire. We lost one man in killed, a Delaware Indian, a brave man and one wounded.

In the morning we started for the Indians, arrived at the place where they had fortified themselves but they had left. On examination of the fort we discovered that during the attack of the previous evening they had lost several. There was blood in the fort and there being a hole in the ice—a great quantity of (it) in the stream—we found where they had disposed of their dead, there being a large trail made from the fort to the hole in the ice.

We knew that the main village of the Blackfeet was not far. Bridger, an old experienced mountaineer, said; "Now, boys, the Indians are close. There will in a short time (be) a party of five or six hundred return to avenge the death of those we had slain and it was necessary for us to be on the look-out." In the course of fifteen days his words were verified.

At the distance of one mile from camp there was a large butte on which during the day on its summit we posted a sentinel. He could command a view of the surrounding country. On the fifteenth day he discovered the Blackfeet marching towards us. They encamped on a large island and immediately commenced making fortifications. They were coming for three days. There were at least 1500 warriors in this spot. We commenced fortifying our position as soon as we knew of their approach. We were confident that they would come in force. Our forts were built strong. Nothing but artillery could do it any damage. We were prepared to receive them. The Indians had constructed one hundred and eleven forts on the evening of the arrival of the last of their reinforcements. They had a war dance. We could hear their songs. We well knew that in the morning they would make the attack. We were prepared. They came, saw the strength and invincibility of our position. They fired a few shots but done no execution and finding that they could not do us any damage by charging our breast works which they declined (to do). They commenced retiring.

We dared them to make the attack. We were only sixty strong, the Indians fifteen hundred, but there was not one of our band but felt anxious for the fight. Nothing could persuade them to attack us. They departed, went about one mile away. All sat in council. In a short time, they arose one half going in the direction of the Crow Indian country and the other taking the course they had come. We remained at our fort till Spring without any further molestation.

We kept our animals in (the) nights, feeding them on cottonwood and in the day, allowed them to graze but well guarded. On the return of Spring (1839) we commenced our hunt, trapped the tributaries of the Missouri to the head of Lewis Fork, and then started for the rendezvous on Green River, near the mouth of Horse Creek, there remained till August and then myself and five others, went to Fort Hall and joined a party of the North-west Fur Company.

Trapped to head of Salmon River, then to Malade and down this same to Big Snake River and up Big Snake. Trapped Goose Creek and Raft River, returned to Fort Hall and disposed of the beaver we caught. Remained there one month and then went and joined Bridger in the Blackfoot country.

After striking the waters of the Missouri, we discovered that there were trappers in advance of us. Fifteen of us left the party for the purpose of overtaking the advance party and find out who they were. Overtook them the same day, found them to be a party of trappers in charge of Joseph Gale,[30] trapping for Captain Wyatt.[31] He informed us that he had lately a fight with the Blackfeet. He had several of his men wounded, among whom was Richard Owens but was nearly well of the wounds received.

In the morning we commenced setting our traps. Knowing that our party would come on our trail, we did not consider it necessary to return and, having accomplished that for which we were sent in advance, we concluded to remain until the arrival of the main party.

The men that had gone out to set traps, after having proceeded about two miles came in contact with a party of Blackfeet, were fired upon and compelled to retreat. They reached camp, the Indians in their rear. We secured ourselves and animals in the brush, then commenced the fight. We, though few in number, had the advantage of being concealed, while our enemy was exposed to view. Our main object was to save our animals.

We fought them the greater part of the day. A great number of Indians were killed. They done all in their power to make us leave our concealment, and finally set fire to the brush. The fire consumed all the outer brush and that under which we remained was not touched. I cannot account for our miraculous escape from the flames. It was the hand of

---

30. Gale—name not quite clear in Mss.
31. Probably Capt. Nathaniel Wyeth a New England man, who led a number of trapping parties.

Providence over us—that was the cause. It could have been nothing else—for the brush, where we were concealed, was dry and easily burned as that which had been consumed.

The Indians, finding that they could not drive us from our concealment, and, from the unerring aim of our rifles, every moment they were losing men then concluded to abandon the attack and departed. As soon as they left we started for our main camp, which was some six miles distant. I presume the Indians discovered the approach of the main party, and, fearing that the firing would be heard, and they surrounded by a considerable force, and but poor prospects of any of them getting away if they remained any longer, was the main cause (of the) retreat.

Gale, seeing that he could not travel with his party, on account of his weakness, joined us, then we moved on to Stinking Creek.

The day we arrived we lost one man, killed by the Blackfeet. That same day, I was about eight miles in advance. I saw at a distance a number of ravens hovering over a particular spot. I concluded to go and see the cause, found the carcass of a bear that had been lately killed by Indians; the trail being fresh and taking the course I wished to pursue, caused me to return. Every day, for eight or ten, we were fired upon by Blackfeet. If a trapper should get a few miles in advance he would be fired upon and have to return. We were surrounded by the Indians, and, finding it impossible to hunt to any advantage, we started for the North fork of the Missouri. Up said (?) stream four days march we overtook a large village of Flathead and Pondrai Indians. A chief of the Flatheads and some of his tribe joined us and we travelled on to Big Snake river for winter quarters, and passed this winter without being molested by the Indians.

In the Spring (1840), Bridger and party started for rendezvous on Green River. Jack Robi(n)son and myself for the Utah country to Robidoux's fort, and there disposed of the furs we had caught on our march.

In the fall (1840) six of us went to Grand River and there made our hunt and passed the winter at Brown's Hole on Green River. In the spring (1841) went back to the Utah country and into the New Park and made the Spring hunt. Returned to Robidoux Fort and disposed of our beaver and remained till September (1841).

Beaver was getting scarce and finding it was necessary to try our hand at something else, "Bill" Williams,[32] "Bill" New, Mitchell, Frederick, a Frenchman and myself, concluded to start for Bent's Fort[33] on the Arkansas. Arrived on the Arkansas about one hundred miles above the fort. Mitchell and New decided to remain. They apprehended no

---

32. Undoubtedly the famous "Old Bill" Williams, one of the most picturesque characters of the early west.
33. Bent and St. Vrain were early traders who established Bent's Fort, so long the center of the fur trade for the Southwest. William Bent was the real proprietor of Bent's Fort though Charles Bent to whom Carson here refers was a partner and brother. Ceran St. Vrain came and went to the fort and eventually had a fort some distance away called Fort St. Vrain. The two latter men had a store established about 1832 in Taos which stood where the Columbian Hotel does now.

Covered Wagons Passing the Carson House.   1925

danger from Indians.   We continued on for the fort, arrived in a few days.

Ten days after our arrival, Mitchell and New came.   They were naked.   The Indians run off all their animals, and stole from them everything they had.

I was kindly received at the fort by Messrs. Bent and St. Vrain offered employment to hunt for the Fort at one dollar per day.   Accepted this offer and remained in their employ till 1842.

I wish I was capable to do Bent and St. Vrain justice for the kindness received at their hands.   I can only say that their equals were never in the mountains.   The former, after the conquest of New Mexico, received the appointment of Governor of the Territory.   In the revolution of 1847, (he) was treacherously killed by Pueblo Indians and Mexicans.   His death was regretted by all that knew him, and for the latter, I can say that all mountaineers look to him as their best friend and treat him with the greatest respect.   He now lives in New Mexico and commands the respects of all American(s) and Mexican(s).

PART II.

1842—1847

It has now been sixteen years, I have been in the mountains. The greater part of that time passed far from the habitations of civilized man, and receiving no other food than that which I could procure with my rifle. Perhaps, once a year, I would have a meal, consisting of bread, meat, sugar and coffee, would consider it a luxury. Sugar and coffee could be purchased at the rendezvous for two dollars per pint, and flour one dollar per pint.

In April 1842, the train of wagons of Bent and St. Vrain were going to the states. I concluded to go in with them. It had been a long time since I had been among civilized people. I went and saw my friends and acquaintances, then took a trip to St. Louis, remained there a few days and was tired of remaining in settlements, took a steamer for the Upper Missouri and, as luck would have it, Colonel Fremont,[34] then a Lieutenant, was aboard of the same boat.

---

34. Col. John Charles Fremont is well known as the greatest explorer of the west during the forties of the past century. He chose to take Carson on three of his expeditions and learned to love and respect the Taos scout. Each helped make the other. Col. Fremont was the man who wrote Washington authorities, "With me Carson and the truth are the same thing!"

In his journal of the expedition of 1843, Col. Fremont wrote of the following affair which will be of interest here. "Riding quietly along over the snow, on the 28th we came suddenly upon smokes rising among these bushes and galloping up we found two huts, open at the top and loosely built of sage, which appeared to have been deserted at the instant; and, on looking hastily around, we saw several Indians on the crest of the ridge near by and several others scrambling up the side. We had come upon them so suddenly that they had been well-nigh surprised in their lodges. A sage fire was burning in the middle; a few baskets made of straw were lying about, with one or two rabbit skins;

He had been in search of Captain Dripps, an old experienced mountaineer, but failed in getting him. I spoke to Colonel Fremont, informed him that I had been some time in the mountains and thought I could guide him to any point he would wish to go. He replied that he would make inquiries regarding my capabilities of performing that which I promised. He done so. I presume he received reports favorable of me, for he told me I would be employed. I accepted the offer of one hundred dollars per month and prepared myself to accompany him. We arrived in Kansas (and) started for the Rocky Mountains. His object was to survey the South pass and take the height of the highest peaks of the Rocky Mts. We travelled the course that is now travelled by California emigrants, to Fort Laramie.

The fall before our arrival at the fort, there was a party of trappers that had joined a village of Snake Indians. They had been attacked by a party of Sioux, in which the latter was defeated and lost several men. For revenge the Sioux had collected a number of warriors (about 1000 lodges) for the purpose of having satisfaction for the damage done them by the Whites and Snakes. There were some

and there was a little grass scattered about, on which they had been lying. "Tabibo-bo"! they shouted from the hills—a word in the Snake langauge, signifying white and remained looking at us from behind rocks. Carson and Godey rode towards the hill, but the men ran off like deer. They had been so pressed, that a woman with two children had dropped behind sage brush near the lodge and when Carson accidently stumbled upon her she immediately began screaming in the extremity of fear and shut her eyes fast to avoid seeing him. She was brought back to the lodge and we endeavored in vain to open a communication with the man. By dint of presents and friendly demonstrations, she was brought to calmness and we found that they belonged to the Snake nation, speaking the language of that people—these may be considered among the human beings the nearest approacned to the animal creation. We have reason to believe that these had never before seen the face of a white man."

Sioux at the Fort. They and the trappers and traders endeavored to persuade Fremont not to proceed,
that he ran a great risk, that in all probability he
would meet the Sioux and that his party would be
destroyed.

Fremont informed them that he was directed
by his government to perform a certain duty, that it
mattered not what obstacles were in his advance,
that he was bound to continue his march in obedience
to his instruction, that he would accomplish that for
which he was sent or die in the attempt; and if he
failed, by losing his party, his Government would
eventually punish those that caused the failure. We
continued our march (and) arrived at the South
Pass.

Fremont accomplished all that was desired of
him and then we returned. Arrived Fort Laramie,
sometime in September.

During the expedition I performed the duties
of guide and hunter. I, at Laramie, quit the employ
of Fremont, he continuing his march for the States
taking nearly the same route as that by which he had
come.

I went to Bent's Fort in January 1843, departed
for Taos. In February of same year got married to
Señorita Josepha Jarimilla,[35] a daughter of Don
Francisco Jaramilla. I remained in Taos till April
then started for the States with Bent and St. Vrain. I
was hunter for the train and continued as such til!

35. She was but fifteen years old. Carson's first wife was an Indian
girl whom he married at Bent's Fort probably about 1838. She died
at the birth of their daughter, Prairie Flower, who grew to woman-
hood, married and went to California where she died.

KIT CARSON'S OWN STORY OF HIS LIFE — page 53.

our arrival at Walnut Creek. There we found encamped Capt. P. St. G. Cook with four companies of Dragoons. He informed us that the train of Armijo and several traders was a short distance in his rear. They had (a) great number of wagons and in the party there was about one hundred men,—Mexicans and Americans. Capt. Cook had received intelligence that a large party of Texans were at the crossing of the Arkansas, awaiting the arrival of the train for the purpose of capturing the same and kill and take prisoners of as many Mexicans as they could, in revenge of (for) of the treatment Armijo had given the Texans[36] when in his power. They concluded to remain (and) sent word to Genl. Armijo of the predicament they was in. The dragoons was only to guard them to the Arkansas and they wished to have Armijo send troops for their protection after the departure of the American troops.

I was spoken to in regard of the carrying the letter to Armijo in Santa Fe. They offered $300.00 for the performance of the duty. I agreed to carry it. I left the train and started for Taos. Had with me Dick Owens, arrived at Bent's Fort, was informed that the Utah Indians were on my route. Owens remained at the Fort, Bent furnished me with a fine horse which I could lead and in case I should fall in with any Indians could mount him and make my escape.

I started, discovered the Indian village without them seeing me, passed them during the night

36. This refers to the outrageous treatment of the men of the Sant Fe-Texas expedition of 1841.

arrived safely at Taos, gave the letter to the Alcalde and he forwarded them to Santa Fe. I was to remain for an answer.

Sometime before my arrival Armijo had sent one hundred Mexican soldiers towards the Arkansas to find out about his train and he was to proceed on after them with six hundred (men).

The first party had reached the Cold Springs, were attacked by Texans and all with the exception of one were killed and taken prisoner by the Texans.[37] He made his escape by having been lucky enough to catch one of the Texan's horses, and made away to report to his general, found him on the march with the six hundred men. But when the Genl. heard of the defeat of his brave soldiers, his heart failed him and he returned for Santa Fe in all haste.

I waited in Taos for four days, received the despatches from Armijo, started for the Arkansas, took with me one Mexican. When two days out, saw a large party of Indians coming towards us, they were Utahs. The Mexican advised me to mount my horse and make my escape that the Indians had no animal that could catch him and as for him, he thought the Indians would not (harm?) him and they in all probability would kill me.

I considered the advice very good and was about to mount my horse. I changed my mind and thought how cowardly it would be for me to desert this man that so willingly offered to sacrifice his life to save mine. I told him no that I would die with him.

37. More did escape than the one Carson mentions.

The Indians were rapidly approaching with one old chief some distance in the advance. He came to me with a smile on his countenance—the old rascal—and proffered me his hand. I proffered mine but, instead of taking my hand, he had caught hold of my rifle, endeavored to take it from me. We tussled for a short time and I made him let go his hold. By this time the remainder had arrived. They kept up among themselves a loud talk. Some would ride about us examining their guns, open their pans, knock the priming of their rifles and many other manouvers endeavoring to frighten us or to induce us to change our positions, that they might fire and kill us before we could return the fire. We watched them closely, determined that the first that would raise his gun should be shot. They remained around us for about a half hour and then seeing but little hopes of their being able to kill us without losing two of themselves, they left.

Continued my journey, arrived in a few days at Bent's Fort without having met with any further difficulty. I was informed by Mr. Bent that the dragoons had caught the Texans, disarmed them, and the train continued on its march without fear, not even considering it necessary to come to the fort.

A few days before my arrival at the Fort (1843), Fremont had passed. He had gone about seventy-five miles. I wished to see him and started for his camp. My object was not to seek employment. I only thought that I would ride to his camp, have a talk and then return. But, when Fremont saw me

again and requested me to join him, I could not refuse and again entered his employ as guide and
hunter.

I was sent back to the Fort to purchase mules, I
bought ten head. Fremont continued on to the Fon-
taine-qui-bouille (soda springs) and went to Bent's
Fort on (the) South Fork of (the) Platte river,
where I joined him.

Major Fitzpatrick, an old, experienced mountaineer, was also in his employ and about forty men.
Here we separated. Fitzpatrick took charge of the
main camp, carts, etc. and went to Laramie. Fremont with fifteen men, myself in the number struck
out up Thompson's Fork and from there to Cache-
la-poudre, and thence through the plains of the Laramie, crossed the North Fork of the Platte below the
New Park, to Sweetwater.

We struck the stream about fifteen miles above
the Devil's Gate,[38] then we travelled about the same
route as is now travelled by emigrants to the Soda
Springs on Bear River. From here Fremont started
to the Salt Lake for its exploration and I went to
Fort Hall for provisions. We were getting out. I
reached the Fort, was well received and furnished all
that I required. I started from the Fort, had one
man with me and joined Fremont at the upper end of
the Salt Lake. We travelled around the East side of
the lake about twenty miles till we could get a fair
view of it. We were in front of the large island of
the Lake and Fremont determined to go to it for the
purpose of examining it. Arranged the India Rub-

<hr>

38. Devil's Gate, Wyoming.

Old Bent's Fort
Courtesy of Col. R. E. Twitchell

ber boat, myself and four others accompanied him.
We landed safely. The island is about fifteen miles
from the mainland. We remained on the island part
of one day and night. We brought with us fresh
water for cooking purposes. Found nothing of any
great importance. There were no springs and it was
perfectly barren. We ascended the mountain and
under (a) shelving rock cut a large cross which is
there to this day.

Next morning started back. Had not left the
island more than a league when the clouds commenced gathering for a storm. Our boat leaking
wind kept one man continually employed at the bel-
lows. Fremont directed us to pull for our lives, if
we do not arrive on shore before the storm commenced we will surely all perish. We done our best
and arrived in time to save ourselves. We had not
more than landed when the storm commenced and in
(an) hour the waters had risen eight or ten feet.

We now took up Bear River till we got above the
Lake. Then crossed to and took up Malade, thence
to Fort Hall[39] where we met Fitzpatrick and party.
Fremont from here took his party and proceeded in
advance. Fitzpatrick keeping in rear some eight
days march and we struck for the mouth of the
Columbia River. Arrived safe at the Dalles on the
Columbia. Fremont took four men and proceeded to
Vancouver's to purchase provisions. I remained in
charge of camp.

39. Fort Hall figures in many a western story. Situated in what is
now Wyoming it served often as a stopping place for emigrant
and trader.

In the meantime Fitzpatrick joined (us). We started for Klamath Lake. A guide was employed and (we) arrived there safe and found a large village of Indians having the same (name?) We had with them a talk. We pronounced them a mean, low-lived, treacherous race, which we found to be a fact when we were in their country in 1846.

Here our guide left us and we struck for California. Our course was through a barren, desolate and unexplored country till we reached the Sierra Nevada which we found covered with snow from one end to the other. We were nearly out of provisions and (to) cross the mountain we must let the consequences be what they may. We went as far in the snow as we possibly could with animals, then was compelled to send them back. Then we commenced making a road through the snow. We beat it down with mallets. The snow was six feet on the level for three leagues. We made snow shoes and walked over the snow to find how far we would have to make a road. Found it to be the distance afore stated.

After we reached the extremity of the snow, we could see in the distance the green valley of the Sacramento and the Coast Range. I knew the place well,[40] had been there seventeen years before. Our feelings can be imagined when we saw such beautiful country.

Having nothing to eat but mule meat, we re-

40. Carson's memory was remarkable. He was now and then not sure of a date but facts never escaped him. An old-timer told of reading Scott's "Lady of the Lake" to him. He enjoyed that very much and asked to have passages reread. The next day he repeated much of the poem. It must be remembered that Carson had little schooling and reading and writing were not easy for him.

turned to the place from which we had sent back our animals and commenced the work of making the road. In fifteen days our task was accomplished. Sent back for the animals. They had, through hunger eaten one another's tails and the leather of the pack saddles, in fact everything they could lay hold of. They were in a deplorable condition and we would frequently kill one to keep it from dying, then use the meat for food.

We continued our march and by perseverance in making the road, (for the wind had drifted the snow and in many places, filled up the path which we had made). We finally got across and then commenced descending the mountain. Then we left Fitzpatrick in charge of the main party. Fremont, myself and five or six men went ahead to Sutter's Fort for provisions.

The second day after leaving Fitzpatrick, Mr. Preus(s),[41] Fremont's assistant got lost. We made a search for him, travelled slowly, fired guns so that he could know where we were. We could not find him. In four days the old man returned. Had his pockets full of acorns, having had no other food since he left us. We were all rejoiced at his return, for the old man was much respected by the party.

We arrived safely at Sutter's Fort, three days after the return to camp of Mr. Preuss. When we arrived at the Fort we were nearly naked and in as poor a condition as men possibly could be. We were

---

41. Preuss was called the artist of the party, made maps, sketches, etc. He was from Germany and accompanied Fremont several times.

well received by Mr. Sutter and furnished in a prince-
ly manner everything we required by him.

We remained about a month at the Fort, made
all the necessary arrangements for our return, having found no difficulty in getting all required.

About the first of April, 1844, we were ready to
depart. During our stay at the Fort two of our
party became deranged, I presume from the effects
of starvation and through receiving an abundance.
One morning one of them jumped up, was perfectly
wild, inquired for his mule. It was tied close to him
but he started to the mountains to look for it. After
some time, when his absence was known, men were
sent in search of him. Looked through all the neighborhood, made inquiries of the Indians but could
hear nothing of him. Remained a few days waiting
his return, but as he did not come in, we departed.
Left word with Sutter to make search and, if possible, find him. He done so, and, sometime after our
departure, he was found, was kept at the Fort and
properly cared for till he got well, and then Mr. Sutter sent him to the States.

We took up the valley of the San Joaquin on our
way home, we crossed the Sierra Nevada and Coast
Range, where they join, a beautiful low pass, continued under the Coast Range till we struck the
Spanish trail,[42] then to the Mohave river, a small
stream that rises in the Coast range and is lost in
the Great Basin, down it to where the trail leaves
the Mohave River (Sentence all but illegible about

---

42. The Spanish trail led directly out from Taos.

their arrival on the Mohave) to our camp. They informed us that they were of a party of Mexicans
from New Mexico. They and two men and women
were encamped a distance from the main party herd-
ing horses that they were a mounted (party). The
two men and women were in their camp, that a party
of Indians charged on them for the purpose of running off their stock. They told the men and women
to make their escape, that they would guard the
horses. They run the animals off from the Indians,
left them at a Spring in the desert about thirty miles
from our camp.

We started for the place where they said they
left their animals, found that they had been taken
away by the Indians that had followed them.

The Mexican requested Fremont to aid him to
retake his animals. He (Fremont) stated to the party
that if they wished to volunteer for such a purpose
they might do so, that he would furnish animals for
them to ride. Godey and myself volunteered with the
expectation that some men of our party would join
us. They did not. We two and the Mexican took the
trail of (the) animals and commenced the persuit.[43]
In twenty miles the Mexican's horse gave out. We
sent him back, and continued on. Travelled during

43. Col. Fremont said of this affair, "The time, place, object and
     numbers considered, this expedition of Carson and Godey may be
     considered among the boldest and most disinterested which the
     annals of western adventure, so full of daring deeds can present.
     Two men, in a savage desert pursue day and night an unknown
     body of Indians into the defiles of an unknown mountain—attack
     them on sight, without counting numbers—and defeat them in
     an instant—and for what? To punish the robbers of the desert,
     and to avenge the wrongs of Mexicans whom they did not know.
     I repeat; it was Carson and Godey who did this—the former as
     American, born in Kentucky; the latter a Frenchman by descent,
     born in St. Louis; and both trained to western enterprise from
     early life."

the night. It was very dark. Had to dismount to feel for the trail. By sign we became aware that the Indians had passed after sunset. We were much fatigued, required rest, unsaddled, wrapped ourselves in the wet saddle blankets and laid down. Could not make any fire for fear of it being seen. Passed a miserably cold night. In the morning we arose very early, went down in a deep ravine made a small fire to warm ourselves, and, as soon as it was light, we again took the trail.

As the sun was rising (we) saw the Indians two miles ahead of us, encamped having a feast. They had killed five animals. We were compelled to leave our horses, they could not travel. We hid them among the rocks, continued on the trail, crawled in among the horses. A young one got frightened, that frightened the rest. The Indians noticed the commotion among the animals (and) sprung to their arms. We now considered it time to charge on the Indians. They were about thirty in number. We charged. I fired, killed one. Godey fired, missed but reloaded and fired killing another. There was only three shots fired and two were killed. The remainder run. I then took the two rifles and ascended a hill to keep guard while Godey scalped the dead Indians. He scalped the one he shot and was proceeding towards the one I shot. He was not yet dead and was behind some rocks. As Godey approached, he raised (and) let fly an arrow. It passed through Godey's shirt collar. He again fell and Godey finished him.

We gathered the animals (and) drove them to

where we had concealed our own, changed horses and drove to camp and safely arrived. Had all the animals, with the exception of those killed (by the Indians) for their feast.

We then marched on to where the Mexicans had left the two men and women. (The) men we discovered dead,—their bodies horribly mutilated. The women, we supposed, were carried into captivity. But such was not the case for a party travelling in our rear found their bodies very much mutilated and staked to the ground.

We continued our march and met no further molestation till we arrived on the Virgin (River), where the trail leaves it. There we intended to remain, our animals being much fatigued. We moved our camp a mile further on.

In looking among the mules, a Canadian of our party, missed one of his mules. He started back for the camp to get it, knowing that it must have been left. He did not inform Fremont or any of the party of his project. In a few hours, he was missed. Those of the horse guard said he had gone to our last camp to look for his mule. I was sent with three men to seek him. Arrived at the camp, he could not be found. (We) saw where he fell from his horse. Great deal of blood was seen. Knew that he was killed. Searched for his body but it could not be found, followed the trail of his animal to where it crossed the river. Returned to camp, informed Fremont of his death. He, in the morning. with a party went to seek the body. Searched some time but without success.

I was grieved on account of the death of the Canadian. He was a brave, noble-souled fellow. I had been in many an Indian fight with him and I am confident, if he was not taken unawares, that he surely killed one or two (Indians) before he fell.

We now left the Virgin, keeping to the Spanish trail, till we passed the Vega of Santa Clara[44] then (we) left the Spanish trail, struck towards the Utah Lake, crossed it and went to the Wint(e)y and thence to Green River, Brown's Hole, then to Little Snake River, to the mouth of St. Vrain's Fork. We then crossed the point of mountain and struck the Laramie River below the New Park. (We) passed the New and on into the Old Park. From there to the Balla Salado, the head waters of the south fork of the Platte, then to the Arkansas River where it leaves the mountains, down it to Bent's fort. We arrived at Bent's fort July, 1844, and remained until after the 4th. Then Fremont and party started for the states and I for Taos.

On the 4th of July, Mr. Bent gave Fremont and party a splendid dinner. The day was celebrated as well, if not better, than in many of the towns of the States.

I arrived in Taos and remained till March, 1845. Dick Owens and I concluded that, as we had rambled enough that it would be advisable for us to go and settle on some good stream and make us a farm. We went to Little Cimmeron, about fifty-five miles east of Taos, built ourselves little huts, put in considerable grain, and commenced getting out timber to enlarge

44. Location of the Vega of Santa Clara is unknown.

our improvements. Remained there till August of same year.

The year previous, I had given my word to Fremont that, in case he should return for the purpose of making any more exploration, that I would willingly join him. He reached Bent's fort about the 1st of August, made inquiries where I was and heard of my being on the Cimmeron. (He) sent an express to me. Then Owens and I sold out for about half it was worth, and we started to join Fremont and we both received employment.

We took up the Arkansas River to where it comes out (of) the mountain, thence to Balla Salado, thence to the Arkansas (above the cañon) and up to its head waters. Then crossed over to Piney River, down it to about 25 miles of its mouth, then to Grand River, crossed, and then to (the) head of White River, down it to near where it empties into Green River. Crossed Green River and went on to the Wint(e)y, up it to near where it comes out of the mountain, left it, crossed the mountains, and on to Provost Fork. It was named so on account of a party of trappers having been defeated on it by a band of Indians. The trappers were under the charge of a man named Provost.[45] His party were all killed with the exception of four.

We took down Provost to the Little Utah Lake, which empties into the Great Salt Lake, followed its outlet to near the Great Salt Lake. Here Fremont made his camp,—some distance south of our former

45. Etienne Provost probably. The name is often written Provo.

encampment. There was in our front a large island, the largest of the lake. We were informed by Indians that on it there was abundance of fresh water and plenty of antelope. Fremont took a few men, I being one, and went to the Island to explore it. We found good grass, water, timber and plenty of game. We remained there some two days killing meat and exploring (the island). It was about fifteen miles long and in breadth about five miles. We then went back to camp.

In going to the Island we rode over salt from the thickness of a wafer to twelve inches. We reached it horseback, kept around the south side of the Lake to the last water. Fremont started Maxwell,[46] Archbeau, Lajeunesse and myself to cross the desert. It had never before been crossed by white man. I was often here. Old trappers would speak of the impossibility of crossing, that water could not be found, grass for the animals, there was none.

Fremont was bound to cross. Nothing was impossible for him to perform if required in his explorations.

Before we started it was arranged that at a certain time of (the) next day we should ascend the mountain near his camp, have with him his telescope, so that we could be seen by him, and if we found grass or water, we should make a smoke, which would be the signal to him to advance. We travelled on about sixty miles (found) no water or grass, not a particle of vegetation could be found, (ground as

---

46. This was Lucien Maxwell. Lajeunesse is a name still living in Taos.

level as a barn floor), before we struck the mountains
on the west side of the Lake. Water and grass was
there in abundance. The fire was made. Fremont
saw it and moved on with his party. Archambeau
started back and me(e)t him when about half way
across the desert. He camped on the desert one
night and next evening at dark, he got across having
lost only a few animals.

Then we separated. Mr. Talbot took charge of
the camp. His guide was Walker. He was ordered
to strike for Mary's River and then follow it down to
where it is lost in the Basin. Fremont took with him
fifteen men to pass south of Mary's River. Both
parties were to meet at the lake made by Carson
River.

We passed over a fine country, plenty of grass
and water, only having about forty miles to travel
without water before reaching the Lake, arrived at
the Lake and waited the arrival of Talbot. In two
days or three days he and party arrived. Here we
again separated, Talbot and Walker to go through a
pass to our south, cross over the Sierra Nevada to
the waters of San Joaquin. We went up Carson
River[47] to Sutter's Fort, having crossed the Sierra
Nevada, arrived safely at the Fort. The old Captain
Sutter was there and was happy to see us and furnished everything we wanted. We remained a few
days, purchased about forty head of cattle and a few
horses, then started to meet our camp. Went up the
San Joaquin valley, crossed, where it comes out of

47. Undoubtedly named after Kit Carson himself but of that he says
nothing.

the mountain and then on to King's River, up to the
head waters. During our march, from snow and
travelling over rocks our cattle became very tender-
footed. From the head of King's River we started
back for the prairie and when we arrived we had no
cattle, they having all given out. Had to leave behind all except those we killed for meat. As we were
getting from the mountains, during the night, some
Indians crawled into our camp and killed two of our
mules. Next morning we started back for the Fort.
Through some mistake we had not found our camp
and, as we had lost nearly all our animals, it became
necessary to return. The same evening we came on
a party of Indians, killed five of them, and continued
on to the Fort. Arrived at the fort safely. All were
afoot, lived principally on the meat of wild horses
that we killed on the march. We now started for San
Jose, only remained a few days to recruit. Got a few
animals and crossed the coast range to see if we
could hear anything of our party under Talbot. At
San Jose we heard that they were on the Joaquin.
Fremont sent me and two men, to meet them. We
met them on the San Joaquin. Guided them to San
Jose.

After we had all got together again we set out
for Monterey to get an outfit. When we arrived
within about 30 miles of Monterey, Fremont received a very impertinent order from General Castro, ordering him to immediately leave the country
and if he did not, that he would drive him out.

We packed up at dark, moved back about 10

miles to a little mountain, found a good place and made a camp. General Castro came with several hundred men and established his headquarters near us. He would frequently fire his big guns to frighten us, thinking by such demonstrations he could make us leave.

We had in the party about forty men armed with rifles, Castro had several hundred soldiers of Artillery, Cavalry and Infantry. Fremont received expresses from Monterey from Americans advising him to leave, that the Mexicans were strong and would surely attack us. He sent them word that he had done nothing to raise the wrath of the Mexican commander, that he was in performance of a duty, that he would let the consequences be what they may, execute a retreat he would not.

We remained in our position on the mountain for three days, had become tired of waiting for the attack of the valiant Mexican General. We then started for the Sacramento River, up it to Peter Lawson's, there Fremont intended getting his outfit for the homeward trip. Remained some ten days.

During our stay at Lawson's, some Americans that were settled in the neighborhood came in stating that there were about 1000 Indians in the vicinity making preparations to attack the settlements, requested assistance of Fremont to drive them back. He and party and some few Americans that lived near started for the Indian encampment. Found them to be in great force, as was stated. They were attacked. The number killed I cannot say. It was a perfect butchery. Those not killed fled in all directions and we returned to Lawson's. Had accomplished what we went for and given the Indians such a chastisement that (it) would be long before they ever again would feel like attacking the settlements.

We remain(ed) some time at Lawson's, received the best of treatment and finished (getting together) our outfit. Started for the Columbia River by going up the Sacramento and passing near the Shasta butte. Traveled on without any molestation, till we reached Klamath Lake at the upper end of it.

A few days after we left, information was received in California that war was declared between the United States and Mexico. Lieutenant Gillespie, U. S. Marines and six men were sent after us to have us come back. He had traveled about three hundred miles. His animals were giving out and the rate he was traveling he had but poor hopes of overtaking us. He then concluded to mount two men on his best animals and send them in advance. They came up to us on the Lake, gave the communications to Fremont, and he having but poor faith in Klamath Indians, feared the situation of Gillespie and party, concluded to go and meet him. Took ten picked men, traveled about sixty miles and met him encamped for the night.

He sat up till 12 or 1 o'clock reading the letters which he had received from the States. Owens and myself were rolled in our saddle blankets laying near the fire, the night being cold. Shortly after Fremont had laid down I heard a noise as of an axe striking, jumped up, saw there were Indians in camp, gave the alarm. The Indians had then tomahawked two men, Basil Lajeunesse and a Delaware and were proceeding to the fire where four Delawares were lying. They heard the alarm. Crane a Delaware got up, took a gun, but not his own. The one he got was not loaded. He was not aware of it (and) kept trying to fire. Stood erect (and) received five arrows in the breast, four mortal. Then (he) fell.

The evening before I fired off my gun for the purpose of cleaning it. (I had) accidentally broken the tube, had nothing but my pistol. Rushed on him, fired, cut the string that held his tomahawk. Had to retire having no other (weapon). Maxwell fired on him, hit him in the leg. As he was turning, Step fired, struck him in the back, ball passing near the heart and he fell. The balance of his party then run. He was the bravest Indian I ever saw. If his men had been as brave as himself we surely would all have been killed. We lost three men and one slightly wounded. If we had not gone to meet Gillespie, he and party would have been murdered. The Indians evidently were on his trail for that purpose. We apprehend(ed) no danger that night and the men being much fatigued no guard was posted. It was the first and last time we failed in posting guard. Of the three men killed Lajeunesse was particularly regretted. He had been with us in every trip that had been made. All of them were brave, good men. The only consolation we had for the loss was that, if we had not arrived, Gillespie and his four men would have been killed. We lost three so two lives had been saved.

After the Indians left, each of us took a tree, expecting that they would return. We remained so posted until daylight. We then packed up, took the bodies of the dead and started for camp of the main party.

(We) had proceeded about ten miles, could not possibly carry the bodies any further. Went about half a mile of (away from) the trail and interred them, covering the graves with logs and brush, so that there was but little probability of their being discovered. (We) would have taken the bodies to our camp, but on account of the timber being so thick, the bodies knocked against the trees and becoming much bruised, concluded to bury them when we did. We met our camp, this evening. They had received orders to follow our trail. Camped for (the) night. Next morning only to go a few miles. Left 15 men in our old camp, concealed for the purpose of discovering the movements of the Indians. We had not left more than half an hour when two Indians came. They were killed and in short time their scalps were in our camp.

Fremont concluded to return to California but (to) take a different route from that (by) which we had last entered the country, by going on the opposite side of the Lake. We were now encamped on a stream of the lake nearly opposite to the place where we were encamped when we had the three men killed. In the morning, I was sent ahead, with ten chosen

men, with orders that, if I discovered any large village of Indians, to send back word and in case I
should be seen by them for me to act as I thought
best.

I had not gone more than ten miles (when) I
discovered a large village of about 50 lodges and, at
the same time, by the commotion in their camp I
knew that they had seen us, and considering it useless to send for reinforcements, I determined to attack them, charged on them, fought for some time,
killed a number and the balance fled.

Their houses were built of flag, beautifully wov-
en. They had been fishing (and) had in their houses
some ten wagon loads of fish they had caught. All
their fishing tackle, camp equipage, etc. was there. I
wished to do them as much damage as I could, so I
directed their houses to be set on fire. The flag being dry it was a beautiful sight. The Indians had
commenced the war with us without cause and I
thought they should be chastized in a summary manner. And they were severely punished.

Fremont saw at a distance the fire, (and) knowing that we were engaged, hurried to join us, but
arrived too late for the sport. We moved on about
two miles from where the Indian village had been,
and camped for the night. After encamping, Owens
and twenty men were sent back to watch for Indians.
In an hour he sent us word that 50 Indians had returned to camp, I suppose to hunt their lost and bury
their dead.

As soon as the information was received Fremont, with six men started to him, taking a route different from that which Owens had taken, so as to keep concealed. As we got near the camp (we) only saw one Indian. As soon as he was seen, we charged him. I was in advance, got within ten feet of him. My gun snapped, he drew his bow to fire on me. I threw myself on one side of my horse to save myself. Fremont saw the danger in which I was, run horse over the Indian throwing him on the ground and before he could recover he was shot. I considered that Fremont saved my life for, in all probability, if he had not run over the Indian as he did, I would have been shot. We could find no more Indians and, fearing that the party seen by Owens had returned to attack our camp, we returned. Arrived but the Indians did not make an attack.

Next morning we struck out for the Valley of the Sacramento about four days march. Maxwell and Archambeau were traveling parallel with the party about three miles distant, hunting. They saw an Indian coming towards them. As soon as the Indian saw them he took from his quiver some young crows that were tied thereon, concealed them in the grass, and continued approaching. As soon as he was within forty yards he commenced firing. They did not intend to hurt him wishing to talk but the Indian keeping up a continuous fire and having shot rather close, they were compelled through self defense to fire on him. They done so and the first shot he fell, was immediately scalped.

We kept on till we struck the Sacramento and

in passing down the river there was ahead of us a deep and narrow cañon. The Indians supposing that we would go through it, placed themselves on each side for the purpose of attacking us as we passed. But we crossed the river and did not go into the cañon.

Godey, myself and another man—I have forgotten his name,—took after them. We were mounted on mules. They could not be caught. One man, brave(r) than the rest, hid himself behind a large rock and awaited our approach. We rode up near him. He came from his hiding place and commenced firing arrows very rapidly. We had to run back, being kept so busy dodging from his arrows, that it was impossible to fire. Retired from the reach of his arrows, I dismounted and fired. My shot had the desired effect. He was scalped. (He) had a fine bow and beautiful quiver of arrows, which I presented to Lt. Gillespie. He was a brave Indian, deserved a better fate, but he had placed himself on the wrong path.

Continued our march and the next day, in the evening, Step and another man had gone out to hunt. We had nothing to eat in our camp, (were) nearly starving. They saw an Indian watching the camp. I presume he was waiting so that he might steal a mule. They gradually approached him,—he was unaware of their presence,—and, when near enough, fired. He, receiving the death wound, was then scalped. The hunters returned having found no other game. We kept on our march to Peter Lawson's, and had no difficulty on the route. Then down

the Sacramento to the Buttes. Here camp was made
to await positive orders in regard to the war to hunt.

A party was sent from here to surprise Sonoma,
a military post. They captured it, took one General
and two Captains prisoners, several cannon and a
number of small arms. After the Fort had been tak-
en, Fremont had heard positively of the war being
declared. (He) then marched forward to Sonoma,
and found it in the possession of the men he had sent
in advance.

During our stay here, General Castro ordered
one of his captains and large force from San Francisco to attack us and drive us from the country. He
came over, found two of our men that were carrying
news to the settlers that Sonoma was taken and war
declared, whom he brutally murdered. He found
that we were anxious to meet him and commenced
his retreat. We followed him some six days and
nights. He could not be found. He made his escape
leaving his animals and he reached San Francisco
and from there went to (the) Pueblo of Los Angeles,
General Castro joining him,—their object being to
reorganize their forces.

Fremont left a strong force at Sonoma. All the
American settlers by this time had joined him. He
then departed for Sutter's fort and arrived safe. He
placed the fort under military command. Left General Vallejos, the two Captains and an American
named Leace (brother-in-law to the General) as prisoners there, in charge of the gentlemen, to whom he
gave the command. (He) then departed to Monterey.
It had been taken before our arrival, by the navy,

under command of Commodore Sloat. A few days
after our arrival Sloat left and Stockton assumed
the command.

Here we learned that General Castro had made
his escape, had gone to Los Angeles to organize. We
found that we could not catch the Mexicans by following them on land, so Fremont proposed, if furnished a frigate to take his men to San Diego, he there
(would) get animals and go drive the Mexican troops
from Los Angeles. The frigate Cyane was furnished
him com'd by Captain Dupont, a noble-souled fellow.
In four days (we) arrived at our destination. Our
forces were landed, 150 strong. Sufficiency of horses could not be procured at San Diego. Men were
sent to scour the country (and to) press into service
horses. We finally were started for Los Angeles.

The Mexicans having heard of our approach,
though they were 700 strong, fled. The Gen., Gov.,
and other officers for Sonora, the balance to all parts
(just) so they did not come in contact with Americans.

We arrived within a league of the town, awaited
a short time and Stockton, agreeable to the plan
arranged (before) our departure from Monterey.
Arrived with a party of sailors and marines. The
sailors and marines were as brave men as I ever saw
and for the Com(m)odore, it is useless for me to say
anything, as he is known to be the bravest of the
brave.

We took possession of the town, remained some
time, and on the 5 Sept. 46 I was ordered to Washington as bearer of despatches, having with me 15 men.

I was ordered to go to Washington in 60 days,[48] which I would have done if not directed by General Kearn(e)y to join him.[49] When I got within 10 miles of the Copper Mines I discovered an Apache village. It was about 10 A. M. They were at war. I knew that by staying where we were we would be seen, and, if we endeavored to pass them, they would also see us. So I had a consultation with Maxwell and we came to the conclusion to take for the timber and approach them cautiously and if we were seen, to be as close as possible to them at the time of the discovery. We kept on, had arrived about 100 yards of the village when they saw us. They were somewhat frightened to see us. We said we were friends, were enroute to New Mexico, wished to trade animals. They appeared friendly. We chose a good place for our camp. They visited us and we commenced trading and procured of them a remount which was much required, our animals all having nearly given out.

We then started and, in four days, arrived at the first of the settlements. At our departure from California we had only 25 lbs. of dried meat, having a quantity of pinola. At the River village we got some corn. We would dry the corn by the fire, parch the corn, then eat it. Not having other food during our trip, we suffered considerably for food.

On the 6th of October, '46, I met General Kearn-

---

48. Carson never quite forgave Gen. Kearney for taking away from him the honor of bearing dispatches to Washington. He was looking forward also to a visit at home after a long absence and as Carson dearly loved his wife and family this disappointment was not slight. It took the soldier heart of a real man thus to obey orders and turn his face westward again.

49. A soldier of the day John T. Hughes wrote of this disappointment, "It requires a brave man to give up his private feelings thus for the public good; Carson was one such." Sen. Doc. 608.

(e)y on his march to California. He ordered me to join him as his guide. I done so and Fitzpatrick continued on with the despatches.

On the 18th (15) of October we left the Rio Del Norte, Decr. 3 (2) arrived at Warner's Ranch, and marched on for San Diego. On the 6th we heard of a party of Californians encamped on our route, probably one hundred in number. When we arrived within ten or fifteen miles of their camp, General Kearn-(e)y sent Lieutenant Hammond with three or four Dragoons ahead to examine their position. He went, was accidently discovered, saw the encampment as reported. They were in an Indian village. He then returned to us and gave the information found. The General then determined to attack them. We picked up about one o'clock in the morning and moved on.

When within a mile of their camp we discovered their spies that were out watching the road and our movements. The trot and then the gallop was ordered to pursue the spies. They retreated to their camp.

I was ordered to join Captain Johnston. He had fifteen men under his command. We were to proceed in advance. Our object was to get the animals belonging to the Californians.

Captain Moore, having a part of two companies of Dragoons and a party of twenty five volunteers that had come from San Diego, was ordered to attack the main body. They were attacked, only fought about ten or fifteen minutes, then they retreated.

When we were within 100 yards of their camp, my horse fell, threw me and my rifle was broken into two pieces. I came very near being trodden to death. Being in advance the whole command had to pass over me. I finally saved myself by crawling from under them.

I then ran on about 100 yards to where the fight had commenced. A Dragoon had been killed. I took his gun and cartridge box and joined in the melee. Johnston and two or three of the dragoons were then killed. The Californians retreated, pursued by Moore for about three quarters of a mile. Moore had about 60 men, mounted on horses, the balance on mules.

Two or three days before, we heard of a party of Californians that were enroute to Sonora. Lieutenant Davidson and twenty-five dragoons and I were sent to surprise them. Done so, and captured 70 or 80 head of animals, from which Moore got some 40 horses that were gentle and on which he mounted his men. The command, in the pursuit, had got very much scattered. The enemy saw the advantage, wheeled and cut off the forty that were in advance, and out of the forty, killed and wounded thirty-six. Captain Moore among the slain, also Lieutenant Hammond. General Kearn(e)y was severely wounded and nearly every officer of (the) command was wounded.

Lieutenant Davidson, in charge of two Howitzers, came up, before he could do anything every one of his party were killed or wounded, and one piece taken by the enemy. They captured it by lassoing the horse, fastening the lasso to the saddle and then

The Home of Carson in Taos
Photograph of 1915

running off. They got about 300 yds. and endeavored to fire it at us, but could not.

It was impossible for Lieutenant Davidson to do anything, having lost all his men, and one piece (of artillery) and was himself lanced several times through the clothing, and one (lance), passing through (the) cantel of his saddle, which if the Californians had not missed his aim he, also, would be numbered among the slain.

We rallied in a point of rocks near where the advance had been defeated, remained there that night, the reason (being we did) not dare to move on, and having a number of dead to bury. The dead were buried at the hours of 12 or 1 o'clock that night. Next day we moved on.

I had command of about 15 men and was ordered in advance. Marched about seven miles. During the night, the Californians had received reinforcements. They were now about 150 strong. During the day they would show themselves on every hill ahead of us.

Late in the evening we (were) still on the march, —being within about 400 yards from the water where we intended to camp. They then charged on us, coming in two bodies, we were compelled to retreat about 200 yards, to a hill of rocks that was to our left. After we had gained our position on the hill, the Californians took another hill about 100 yds. still to our left, and then commenced firing. Captains Emery and Turner took the command of what dragoons we had.

charged the enemy on the hill, routed them, giving us full possession of their position, there remained for the night.

The day on which we had the first fight, Kearn-(e)y had sent three men as express to San Diego to Com(m)odore Stockton. This morning they had returned. Within five hundred yards of our camp they were taken prisoners by the enemy in our sight. The day previous, the horse of a Mexican Lieutenant was shot and he (was) taken prisoner. The parley was sounded and then exchanged the Lieutenant for one of our men that was prisoner.

The place in which we were stationed had barely water enough for the men to drink. We had nothing to eat but mule meat. The animals were turned loose. As soon as any would get from the reach of our guns they would be driven off by the enemy. The Mexicans had command of the water, probably about 500 yds. in our advance. Kearn(e)y concluded to march on let the consequences be what they would. About 12 o'clock we were ready to march, the wounded in ambulances (in litters on mule back). The enemy, seeing our movements, saddled up, formed in our rear 500 yards, the men being placed about 10 feet apart so that our artillery could do them but little damage.

Kearn(e)y had a council with his officers. They all knew that, as soon as we would leave the hill, we would again have to fight and, in our present condition, it was not advisable. They came to the conclusion to send for reinforcements to San Diego. Lieutenant Beale, of the navy, and myself, volunteered to undertake to carry the intelligence to Stockton.

As soon as dark we[50] started on our mission. In crawling over the rocks and brush our shoes making noise, we took them off; fastened them under our belts. We had to craw about two miles. We could see three rows of sentinels, all a horseback. We would often have to pass within 20 yards of one. We finally got through, but had the misfortune to have lost our shoes, had to travel over a country covered with prickly pear and rocks, barefoot.

Got to San Diego the next night.[51] Stockton immediately ordered 160 or 170 men to march to Kearn-(e)y's relief. They were under the command of a Lieutenant, (had) one cannon, which was drawn by the men by attaching to it ropes.

I remained at San Diego, Lieutenant Beale was sent aboard of frigate Congress, had become deranged from fatigue of the service performed. Did not entirely recover for two years.

The next night the reinforcements reached Kearn(e)y. They lay by during the day, traveled by night. The enemy, however, discovered their approach then fled. Kearn(e)y and party then joined and moved on to San Diego having no further molestation. Remained in San Diego about a month or so, till the wounded recovered. Then a force of 600 men were organized and started for Los Angeles

50. Lt. Edward Fitzgerald Beale was with Carson.
51. This feat so modestly told here may easily be considered one of the greatest of its kind in all United States History. Carson suffered much following this daring exploit but of this he says nothing. To save others from annihilation he risked his life. Lt. Beale and the Indian, whose name we do not know, share the honors. It is said the Indian reached San Diego first, then Carson and Beale.

under Stockton and Kearn(e)y.   There were at Los
Angeles about 700 Mexicans.

On the 8th day January 47, we arrived within
15 miles of Los Angeles. The Mexicans had a good
position, being in command of a hill where we had to
pass the river. We had two pieces of cannon. Stockton directed them. The Mexicans only stood a few
rounds of fire, retreated and crossed the river, took
possession of the hill and encamped for the night.

On the 9th we approached within three miles of
the Pueblo, having to fight during the day. Nothing,
however, was necessary to be employed but the artillery. They could not make their appearance near us
but Stockton from his unerring aim of his guns
would make them leave.

On the 10th we took possession of the Pueblo.
The place was evacuated by the Mexicans.   They
went to attack Fremont. He was thirty (miles) distant from the Pueblo. On the march thither with
about 400 men that he had raised in the vicinity of
Monterey. They met him, would not fight him, sur-
rendered to him in preference to any other of the
commanders.

On the 12th, I think, Fremont found us at Los
Angeles. We remained there during the winter
without any further molestation. As soon as Fremont joined, I left Kearn(e)y and joined him.[52]   In
March, I started as bearer of dispatches for the War
Dept. Lieutenant Beale went with me with dispatches for the Navy Dept.

<hr />

51. This is not hard to understand. Kearney robbed Carson of the
honor of carrying the messages to Washington as well as a visit
to his family in Taos on the way. The much greater man Fremont
had the affection and respect of Carson.

Beale, during the first 20 days, I had to lift him on and off his horse. I did not think he could live, but I took as good care and paid to him as much attention as could (be) given to anyone in the same circumstances, and, before our arrival he had got so far recovered that he could assist himself. For my care, I was trebly repaid by the kindness and attention given me by his mother while I was in Washington.

On the River Gila, we were attacked by the Indians. During (the) night they sent a good many arrows into our camp, but without effect. As soon as they commenced, I directed the men to hold before them pack saddles and not to speak a word, so that the Indians could not direct their aim by hearing us, for them not to return the fire but let the Indians approach, and then use our rifles as clubs.

The Indians did not approach but, finding they done no execution they left before morning. And we continued our journey. Had no further difficulty and arrived at Washington in June.

At St. Louis, I had the honor of an introduction to Colonel Benton and was invited by him that during my stay in Washington to remain at his home. I accepted of his invitation and, during the time I was there, received the very kindest of treatment.

I remained in Washington some time, received the appointment of Lieut. of Rifles U. S. Army from President Polk and was ordered back to California as bearer of dispatches. Lt. Beale (went) with me, but, on account of his illness, he was compelled to return from St. Louis.

When I arrived at Fort Leavenworth I was furnished an escort of fifty men, volunteers, the Commanche Indians being at war. I came on to Pawnee Rock without any difficulty. Was encamped about 300 yards from a company of Volunteers enroute for New Mexico having with them a very large train of wagons.

At daylight the men of said company were leading out their horses to picket them in new grass. They were attacked by a party of Commanches and had 26 horses and all their cattle driven off. The cattle taking a turn near our camp, I was enabled to retake them from the Indians. I lost two horses but through fault of my men having the rope in their hands and wishing to fire at the Indians, they let the horses go.

The company lost 26 and would have lost all of their cattle, if I and my party had not been there to assist them. Also had three men wounded. I lost two horses as before stated. The volunteers were under the command of Lieutenant Mulony (Maloney?)[53]

We then continued our march and arrived at Santa Fe without any difficulty. There I left my escort and hired sixteen men and continued my journey to California. At Muddy Creek a tributary of the Virgin River, there were about 300 Indians collected. They wanted to come into my camp. I would not permit them. I told them that the fall be-

___

53. C. L. Camp suggests this name. See page 8.

fore they had killed seven Americans, that they were
of a treacherous character and could not be trusted
and that I would not allow myself to be deceived by
them, that their object was to come to me friendly
and then kill my party. I told them to retire, if not
I would fire on them.

I was compelled to fire. One Indian was killed
and the balance went off. I had no more trouble on
the road, only having got out of provisions and had
to eat two mules.

Arrived at Los Angeles in October, then went on
to Monterey and delivered the dispatches to Colonel
Mason and the Drags officer in command. Remained
a few days and was ordered back to Los Angeles.

Shortly after my arrival (at Los Angeles) I was
assigned to duty with the Dragoons under command
of Captain Smith. The greater part of the winter,
I passed in the Tejon Pass. Had twenty five men
under my command guarding the Pass, to prohibit
Indians from taking through stolen animals. It being the main pass, they would have (to) go through
in case they committed any depredations.

In the Spring I was again ordered to Washington as bearer of dispatches. I reached Grand River
without any serious difficulty. Then, the river being
high, I lost in rafting it, one raft which had on it six
rifles and a number (of) riding and pack saddles.
Lieutenant Brewerton[54] was with me. It was near

---

54. Brewerton greatly admired Carson. Among other interesting
paragraphs we find this in his account of the trip of 1848:
    "During the journey I often watched with great curiosity
Carson's preparations for the night. A braver man than Kit
perhaps never lived, in fact, I doubt if he ever knew what fear
was, but with all this he exercised great caution. While arrang-
ing his bed, his saddle which he always used as a pillow, was

sundown when the raft was lost. Some of men were on the opposite bank, the Lieutenant among the number. They were nearly naked, had to remain in that situation during the night and in the morning I sent a man over to them with an axe so that they could make another raft. They, after some labor, made one and crossed. We then continued our march. Some of the men having to ride bareback until we arrived at Taos.

About fifty miles of Taos we met several hundred Utah and Apache Indians. They showed demonstrations of hostility. We retired into the brush, would only allow a few of them to approach us, informed them that, if they were friends, that they should leave, that we were naked and in a destitute condition and could give them nothing. They evidently left us, when they saw we had nothing.

That night I moved on about ten miles and met a party of volunteers on their pursuit of the Apaches. Next day reached Taos, then to Santa Fe, found Colonel Newby, of Illinois Volts. in command. He rendered me all the assistance I required, informing me that the Commanches were still at war and were in parties of from two and three hundred watching the roads.

---

disposed in such a manner as to form a barricade for his head, his pistols half cocked, were laid above it, and his trusty rifle reposed beneath the blanket by his side, where it was not only ready for instant use, but perfectly protected from the damp. Except now and then to light his pipe, you never caught Kit exposing himself to the full glare of the camp fire. He knew too well the treacherous character of the tribes among whom we were traveling, he had seen men killed at night by an unseen foe, who veiled in darkness, stood in perfect security while he marked and shot down the mountaineer clearly seen by the firelight, 'No, no boys', Kit would say, 'Hang around the fire if you will, it may do for you if you like it, but I don't want to have a Digger slip an arrow into me, when I can't see him.' "

I discharged all my men but ten, retaining the best and then returned to Taos and departed for the States.

Keeping north of the Commanche range, I reached Bijoux, a tributary of the Platte (and traveling) down it to within twenty five miles of the south Fork of the Platte, left the Bijoux River and struck for the Platte, kept down it to Fort Kearney, then struck for the Republican Fork and from thence to Fort Leavenworth, having had no trouble on the march. Thence to Washington and delivered my dispatches. Returned to St. Louis. Remained a few days and started back for New Mexico. Arrived there in October 1848.

When I reached Santa Fe, when on my way to Washington with dispatches, I was informed by Colonel Newby that my appointment of Lieutenant was not confirmed by the Senate and I was advised by many of my friends to deliver to the commanding officer the dispatches and not take them through. I considered the matter over and as I had been entrusted with the dispatches—chosen as the most competent person to take them, through safely—I determined to fulfill the duty.[55]

That mattered not to me if, in the discharge of duty of service beneficial to the public, whether I was of the rank of Lieutenant or holding the credit of an experienced mountaineer. Having gained much honor and credit in performance of all duties entrusted

---

55. This was decidedly characteristic of Carson. Naturally, he was cut to the quick by the news. In 1865, Congress made Carson Brevet Brigadier General. His splendid record during the Civil War forced recognition of his ability as a military leader.

to my charge, I would on no account wish to forfeit the good opinion of a majority of my countrymen because the Senate of the United States did not deem it proper to confirm on me an appointment of an office that I never sought, and one which, if confirmed, I would have (to) resign at the termination of the war.

I was with Fremont from 1842 to 1847. The hardships through which we passed I find it impossible to describe and the credit to which he deserves I am incapable to do him justice in writing. But his services to his country have been left to the judgment of impartial freemen and all agree in saying that his services were great and have redounded to his honor and that of his country.

I have heard that he is enormously rich. I wish to God that he may be worth ten times as much more. All that he has or may ever receive, he deserves. I can never forget his treatment of me while in his employ and how cheerfully he suffered with his men when undergoing the severest of hardships. His perseverance and willingness to participate in all that was undertaken, no matter whether the duty was rough or easy, is the main cause of his success. And I say, without fear of contradiction, that none but him could have surmounted and succeeded through as many difficult services.

PART III.

1847—1857

I remained at Taos during the winter. I made two trips during the time with Colonel Beall in command of the troops and drags in pursuit of Indians.

The Colonel had ordered a command, previous to his departure to pursue the Indians, to cross the mountains. They had advanced some distance and found it impracticable to cross. The officer in the command was advised by his guides to return, that it was utterly impossible to proceed. He returned, reported to Colonel Beall the impracticability of the route,—the cause of his return. The Colonel replied that there was no such word as "impracticable" in the soldier's vocabulary and that nothing ought to be impossible for the I Dragoons to accomplish. He, immediately assumed the command, I was employed as his guide and departed and after surmounting many difficulties and passing through severe hardships, we finally accomplished the object of the expedition, and returned to Taos.

On our return after passing through the Sangre de Cristo Pass an Apache village was discovered. Two chiefs were captured. The Colonel held a talk with them. They made promises of peace and friendship and were liberated. We then continued on and arrived at Taos. Remained till February (when) Colonel Beall heard (that) a large number of In-

dians were encamped on the Arkansas agreeable to
treaty made by United States and Mexico, the former was supposed to deliver to Mexico all the Mexican
captives held by Indians of the former nation. It
was the intention of the Colonel to visit those Indians, to endeavor to have them deliver up all Mexicans held captive—peaceably if he could, forcibly if
he must. His command consisted of two companies
of dragoons and I was his guide.

We arrived at the Arkansas and found encamped there, four nations of Indians, some two
thousand souls. He stated to the Indian agent the
object of his having come there and was informed
that it would be useless to demand of them the captives, at present, that they would surely refuse and
force would be necessary to make them comply with
it and the Indians being in such force that he would
fail in his object if he undertook to fight with such
numbers against him.

It took a great deal of persuasion to cause the
Colonel to desist from making the attempt but, as
the Agent, traders and officers of his command were
opposed to his attempting to make them give up the
captives with such (an) inferior force at his command, he finally concluded not to demand the prisoners but leave it for some other day. That the object
in all probability would be gained by having a treaty
with them and the delivery of the captives, one of the
articles.

We then marched up the Arkansas to the mouth
of the Huerfano, then through the Sangre de Cristo
Pass, thence to Taos.

In April, Mr. Maxwell and I concluded to make
a settlement on the Rayado. We had been leading a
roving life long enough and now was the time, if ever,
to make a home for ourselves and children. We
were getting old and could not expect to remain any
length of time able to gain a livlihood as we had
been such a number of years. Arrived at Rayado,
commenced building and making improvements, and
were in a way of becoming prosperous.

In October, the train of a Mr. White[56] was attacked by the Jicarilla Apache. He was killed and
his wife and child taken prisoner. A command was
organized in Taos, Leroux and Fisher as guides.
When they reached Rayado, I was employed as one
of the guides. We marched to where the depredation had been committed, then took their trail. I was
the first man that found the camp where the murder
had been committed. Found trunks that were brok-
en open, harness cut, and everything destroyed that
the Indians could not carry with them.

We followed them some ten or twelve days. It
was the most difficult trail that I ever followed. As
they would leave the camps, they (would break up)
in numbers (of) from one to two (and travel) in different directions to meet at some appointed place.
In nearly every camp we would find some of Mrs.
White's clothing, which was the cause of renewed
energy to continue the pursuit.

We finally came in view of the Indian Camp. I
was in advance, started for their camp, calling to

56. See "Uncle Dick" Wooton's account of this attempt at rescue.
Conrad, Uncle Dick Wooton, 1891.

the men to follow. The comdg officer ordered a halt, none then would follow me. I was informed that Leroux, the principal guide, told the officer in command to halt, that the Indians wished to have a parley.

The Indians, seeing that the troops did not intend to charge on them, they commenced packing up in all haste. When the halt was ordered the comdg officer was shot; the ball passing through his coat, guantlets that were in his pockets, shirts, and to the skin, doing no serious damage, only making him a little sick at the stomach. The guantlets saved his life leaving to the service of his country, one (man) gallant officer.

As soon as he recovered from the shock given him by the ball, he ordered the men to charge, but the order was too late for the desired effect. There was only one Indian in the camp, he running into the river hard by was shot. In about 200 yards, pursuing the Indians, the body of Mrs. White was found, perfectly warm, had not been killed more than five minutes, shot through the heart with an arrow. She evidently knew that some one was coming to her rescue. She did not see us, but it was apparent that she was endeavoring to make her escape when she received the fatal shot.

I am certain that if the Indians had been charged immediately on our arrival, she would have been saved. The Indians did not know of our approach and perhaps, not paying any particular watch of her, she could (have) run towards us, the Indians fearing to pursue. She could not possibly have lived long for the treatment she had received from the Indians was so brutal and horrible that she could possibly last but a short period. Her life, I think, should never be regretted by her friends. She is surely far more happy in heaven, with her God, than among the friends on this earth.

I do not wish to be understood as attaching any blame to the officer in command or (the) principal guide. They acted as they thought best for the purpose of saving the life of Mrs. White. We merely differed in opinion at the time. But I have no doubt but they now can see that, if my advice had been taken, the life might have been saved, for at least a short period, of the much lamented Mrs. White.

We, however, captured all their baggage and camp equipage. Many running off without any of their clothing, and some animals. We pursued the Indians for about six miles on a level prairie. One Indian was killed and two or three Indian children taken prisoner. I have much regretted the failure of the attempt to save the life of so greatly esteemed and respected a lady.[57]

In camp was found a book, the first of the kind I had ever seen, in which I was made a great hero, slaying Indians by the hundred and I have often thought that as Mrs. White would read the same and knowing that I lived near, she would pray for my appearance and that she might be saved. I did come but had not the power to convince those that were in

---

57. This attempt at rescue was one long remembered in Taos. It was a matter of much discussion as it seemed evident to all that a blunder had been made by the commanding officer. Army men rarely wished to follow the suggestions of mountaineers.

command over me to pursue my plan for her rescue.
They would not listen to me and they failed. I will
say no more regarding the matter, attach no blame to
any particular person, for I presume the consciences
of these that were the cause of the failure has severely punished them ere this.

On the return we had the severest snow storm
that I ever experienced. Had one man frozen to
death. We were trying to make Barclay's fort on
the Mora but, on account of the wind, we could not
keep our course, but happily arrived at some timber
near Las Vegas, in which we were able to take refuge. I learned that in the same storm many of the
Indians that we had been pursuing perished. After
the storm we went in to Las Vegas. Captain Judd
was in command of the post and from there the
command marched to Taos and I proceeded to Rayado, where I remained till Spring.

During the winter there was a detachment of ten
dragoons commanded by Leigh Holbrook stationed
at the Rayado. Sometime during the month of
March a party of Indians came and attacked the
rancho about two miles distant where we had our
animals that were gentle, kept to graze. There were
two men in charge; both were severely wounded.
One, however, made his way to the Rayado and gave
the report. The Dragoons, three Americans, and
myself immediately saddled up and proceeded to the
rancho. It was night when we arrived. Remained
until morning, then took the trail of the animals
that was driven off, followed it at a gallop for 25
miles and discovered at a distance, the Indians. Dur-

Taos Country
Blanche C. Grant
Courtesy of Owner, A. M. Ellis, Los Angeles

ing the pursuit some of our animals gave out and
were left on the trail.

We approached the Indians cautiously and, when
close, charged them, killed five, the other four made
their escape.   We recovered the stolen animals
(with the exception of four) and then returned. Two
of the men with me at the time (have) since being
(been) killed by the same tribe of Indians; Sergt
Holbrook, a gallant and brave soldier was killed in
the battle of Ceneguilla in 1854, and William New, a
brave and experienced trapper was killed at the
Rayado a few months after our pursuit of the Indians
that had stolen the animals from the Rayado.

On the 5 May 1850. Tim Goodel (probably Tim
Goodale) and I started to Fort Laramie with forty
or fifty head of mules and horses to trade with the
emigrants.   Arrived about the first of June, remained about a month, disposed of our animals to
good advantage.   Then we separated, Goodel going
to California, I for my home.   Arrived at the Green-
horn, a tributary of the Arkansas, had with me one
Mexican boy. I learned there that the Apaches were
on the road which I had to travel watching it for the
purpose of murdering those that might pass, I remained about six days to recruit my animals, I could
get no one to accompany me but one man, Charles
Kinney and then started.

The first night I travelled about forty miles
through the mountains, reached the River Trinchero.
Had the animals concealed in the brush, some distance from the road and I ascended the highest cottonwood tree for the purpose of watching for the In-

dians. I remained in that position during the entire day. Sometimes I would fall asleep and nearly fall but would recover in time and continue my watch. Near evening I saw a large body of Indians one half mile distant. They had not as yet discovered our trail. I descended the tree. We saddled up, and proceeded on our journey, keeping in the brush some distance of(f) the road till dark. Then I took the road and travelled to Red River, got there at daylight in the morning and that evening went to Taos. Remained a few days and departed for the Rayado.

During my absence the Indians had run off every head of stock on the Rayado. Troops were stationed there at the time but the Indians came in such force that they feared to attack them. Shortly afterwards there was a command sent in pursuit commanded by Major Grier. They killed some of the Indians and recovered all the stock except that which had been killed by the Indians.

I remained at the Rayado till fall, nothing having transpired of any moment, except my following of an American that had organized a party for the purpose of murdering on the plains, Mr. Saml. Weatherhead and Mr. Elias Brevort, that were supposed to have a large amount of money. Fox was the name of the leader. The object of the party was discovered by Fox, when in Taos, trying to get a man to join him. He stated to him that which was to be done. He refused to go and when he thought Fox had gone sufficient distance not to be apprehended, he stated what Fox had informed him.

Lieut. Taylor, I Dragoons was in Taos at the time (and) came to me saying that he wished Fox apprehended for debt and requested me to pursue him for that purpose. I refused. Then he stated the true cause of his wishing him apprehended which was that he (Fox) and a party of men were travelling in company with Mr. Weatherhead and Brevort, and that it was their intention to murder them as soon as they reached the Cimaron, then go to Texas. I immediately agreed to go when I knew their object. Ten dragoons was given to me. The second night we marched on till one o'clock. Met Captain Ewell in command of recruits enroute for New Mexico. Stated to him the object of the journey. He then joined me with twenty five men.

Came to the camp of Mr. Weatherhead and Brevort, entered it cautiously, arrested Fox, remained there that night. Captain Ewell then took charge of Fox and returned to his camp. Weatherhead and Mr. Brevort then selected fifteen men of his party, in whom he had confidence and directed the remainder to leave. There were about fifty men of their party. I have not the least (doubt) but that they would have been murdered if these men had not been driven away from their party.[58]

---

58. In an unpublished account of an interview with Brevoort, we find the following: "Before leaving camp I and my friends surrounded Kit Carson and acknowledged him as our preserver and wanted to give him what we could in return. He modestly declined and casting his eyes toward heaven said in substance that if there was merit in what he had done he had but done his duty, and if he deserved reward and there was a God in heaven, He would reward him in the great future. Not an eye was dry as he spoke, and even now the tears well up as I think of the man and his words."

Later Brevoort says, "Kit Carson (Christopher) deserves the reputation and credit of subduing the Indians with his New Mexico volunteers; he was naturally a commander. Personally he was

They told me that anything I would ask of them would be freely given, but I demanded nothing for my trouble considering having done a good act thereby saving the lives of two valuable citizens was reward sufficient. However in the Spring following, they made me accept as a present a pair of splendid silver mounted pistols.[59]

I returned to Rayado with Fox, turned him over to the proper authorities. He was then taken to Taos and confined there; but nothing positive could be proven against him and he was liberated.

I remained in Rayado till March and then started for St. Louis, took with me twelve wagons of Mr. Maxwell for the purpose of bringing out goods for him. Arrived at Kansas May 1. I proceeded to St. Louis, purchased the goods, then returned to Kansas loaded the wagons and started for home. I concluded to take the Bent's Fort trail on account of water and grass being in greater abundance thereon.

About fifteen miles above the crossing of the Arkansas, I fell in with a village of Cheyenne Indians. They were at the time hostile to the United

---

mild, rather effeminate voice, but when he spoke his voice was one that would draw the attention of all; everybody would stop to listen. His language was forcible, slow and pointed, using the fewest words possible. He talked but little, was very quiet, and seldom used immoral or profane language; sometimes when greatly excited he would swear, but not generally; he was not a dissipated man. Everybody admired him; he was mild and very affectionate in disposition. He had a special influence over Indians. No one would think of trifling with such a man. He was a very cautious man, which sometimes made people accuse him of cowardice; he was very superstitious. I have known him to fire at a deer only 30 or 40 paces off, a magnificent shot. It never moved; he retraced his steps and felt as though he had fired at an animal that bore a charmed life; nothing could induce him to fire again though the camp was starving for meat. More latterly he wouldn't start on a trip on Friday." Mss. Bancroft Library, Berkeley, California.

59. One of these is now owned by Christopher Carson III, the son of Kit Carson's son William, who now lives in Alamosa, Colo.

States, on account of one of the officers of Colonel
Summer's command (that was about ten days march
in my advance) having flogged an Indian Chief of
their tribe. The cause to me (was) unknown, but I
presume courage was oozing from the finger ends
of the officer, and, as the Indians were in his power,
he wished to be relieved of such (a) commodity.

As an Indian very seldom lets pass an injury
done him unavenged, and it matters not who may be
the victim so that it is of the same nation, I, un-
fortunately, happened to be the first American that
passed them since the insult was given them. On me
they intended to retaliate.

I had travelled about twenty miles from their
village. They pursued me. I was encamped. They
came to me by one, two, and threes till twenty
arrived. I thought them friendly, not having known
that which had been done them. Wished to treat
them with kindness and invited them to sit down and
smoke and talk. They done so. They then commenced talking among themselves and I understood
them to say that, while I would be smoking and not
on my guard, they could easily kill me with a knife,
and, as for the Mexicans with me, they could kill
them as easily as buffalo.

I was alarmed. I had but fifteen men,—two
Americans and thirteen Mexicans, of the latter I had
(a) poor opinion of their bravery in case I should be
attacked. I informed the Indians that I knew not
the cause of their wishing my scalp, that I had done
them no injury and wanted to treat them kindly, that
they had come to me as friends, that I now discovered

that they wished to do me injury and that they must
leave, any refusing would be shot and if they attempted to return that I would fire on them.

They departed and joined those that were in
sight on the hills. I then ordered my men to hitch
up and commence our march. We moved on, the
drivers carrying in one hand their rifles and in the
other their whips. I travelled on till dark, encamped
and started an express to the Rayado.

Next morning I moved on till 12 o'clock, stopped
at noon and five Indians, approaching my camp, I
ordered them to halt when within 100 yards but I
eventually let them come in so that I could speak
more freely to them. As soon as they came in, I informed them that I had the night before sent an express to Rayado, that he had gone for the troops that
were stationed there, and that among them I had
many friends, that they would surely come to my relief, that, if I were killed, they would know by whom
and that my death would be avenged.

They departed, examined the road, and, finding
that all I said was true, and (that) he (the express)
had advanced so far that they could not overtake
him, they concluded to leave me, fearing the arrival
of the troops.

I am confident that I and my party would have
been killed by the Cheyennes (for there were a large
number around me) if I had not sent forward for
assistance, and the only reason they had of attacking
me was, as I afterwards learned, the difficulty among
them caused by the conduct of an officer of Colonel
Summer's command.

My express reached Colonel Summer the third
day, gave to the Colonel the letter which he had but
(as he) would send me no aid, the express continued
on and arrived at Rayado the next day. My letter
was given to Major Grier, the commanding officer.
He immediately detailed Lieutenant Johnston and a
party of men to march to my aid. When Lieutenant
Johnston met Summer he asked him where he was
going, was informed to my aid, the conscience of the
gallant old Colonel then I presume troubled him. He
had refused me aid two days previous and in all
probability I and my party was murdered· He concluded to send Major Carleton and thirty men with
him. That Johnston, a noble and brave officer could
meet the Indians, have a fight and all knew that, if
such was the case, the affair would be properly man-
aged and that he would receive great praise. The
Colonel wished to have a hand in the matter, (so) he
concluded to send Carleton. But to the Colonel I do
not consider myself under any obligations, for two
days previously by his conduct he showed plainly
that by rendering aid to a few American citizens in
the power of Indians, enraged by the conduct of some
of his command, was not his wish.

But I am thankful to Carleton and Johnston
(for) by the kindness they showed me on their arrival and by their anxiety and willingness to punish the
Indians, that wished to interrupt me. Major Grier,
a gentleman and a gallant soldier, is entitled to my
warmest gratitude for the promptness in which he
rendered assistance and cordially showed his cap-
ability of performing the high duty to which he was

appointed. It plainly showed his noble heart and that reliance can be placed in him on the hour of danger.

The services of the troops were not required, for the Indians knew they would come, so, on their arrival they were not in striking distance. The troops came up to me, about twenty miles of Bent's Fort. They returned, I in company with them to Rayado. I then delivered to Mr. Maxwell the wagons and goods and remained till March.

Mr. Maxwell and I rigged up a party of eighteen men to go trapping, I taking charge of them. We went to the Balla Salado, then down the South Fork to the Plains, through the Plains of Laramie to the New Park, trapped it to the Old Park, trapped it again then again to the Balla Salado, then on the Arkansas where it goes out of the mountain, then followed on under the mountain, thence home to the Rayado, through to the Raton Mountain, having made a very good hunt.

I remained at Rayado during the fall and winter. In February '53, I went to the Rio Abajo and purchased sheep. Returned with them to the Rayado. Then I started for California. There was with me, Henry Mercure, John Bernavette and their employees. We had about 6,500 head of sheep.[60]

Went to Fort Laramie, then kept the wagon road that is travelled by emigrants to California, arrived about the first of August, having met with no serious

60. This trip brought Carson real money. He was independent from this time on.

loss. Sold our sheep to Mr. Norris at $5.50 a head doing very well.

I heard so much talk of the great change that had taken place at San Francisco, I concluded to go down and when I arrived, I would not have known the place if I had not been there so often before.

Maxwell came on shortly after me to California. Disposed of his sheep in Sacramento. But on Carson River he sent to me an express, requesting me to await his arrival and then we would travel together home by way of the Gila. He arrived. I went down to Los Angeles by land. He took the steamer. I would not travel on the sea, having made a voyage on that in 1846 and was so disgusted with it, that I swore that it would be the last time I would leave sight of land when I could get a mule to perform the journey. Arrived safely at Los Angeles. Maxwell having arrived some fifteen days before me. Made the necessary preparations and then started for New Mexico.

Came to the Pima village and, on account of the scarcity of grass, we continued up the Gila to the mouth of the San Pedro, up it three days and from there we took a straight course for the copper mines and then (on to) the Del Norte, thence home through the settlements of the Rio Abajo. Arrived at Taos on Decr. 25th. 1853.

On my way home, I saw the Mormon delegate to Congress and by him I was informed that I had received the appointment of Indian Agent. After my arrival at Taos, I accepted the appointment giving the necessary bond.

In February, 1854, the Jicarilla Apache Indians showed a disposition of hostility. Lieut. Beall 2d Dragoons had a fight with them on the waters of Red River, in which there was one or two soldiers killed and some wounded but, in the affray, he killed a number of Indians and they retreated. He had charged them once or twice and they could not stand although they were superior in number.

In March I proceeded to Santa Fé on business[61] pertaining to my office. Before my departure a large party of Jicarilla Apaches had come within twenty miles of Taos. I had seen a number of Chiefs and they all pretended friendship, but, during my absence they became hostile. Lieut. J .W. Davidson I Dragoons and sixty Dragoons of F and I Companies were ordered against them. He overtook them in the Embudo Mountains about 20 miles southwest of Taos. The Indians evidently from the preparations they had made and having chosen such an advantageous position intended to fight the troops sent against them if they did not come in force.

Lieutenant Davidson had sixty men and there were seventy five or eighty lodges of Indians. He marched to them. They immediately saw his small force and surely came to the conclusion to fight for, when a few men were sent in advance, they did not speak to them in a friendly manner and showing demonstrations of hostility, Lieut. Davidson was

---

61. Records of the Masonic Lodge of Santa Fé show that it was at this time that Carson became a Mason.

compelled to attack them. I know Davidson well, having been in engagements when he done a prominent part and I know him to be as brave as officer can be and from the men that were in the engagement of that day I have been informed that during the fight he never took ambush and that when in retreat, he directed his men to take shelter as best they could but that he, fearing no danger, remained exposed to the fire of the Indians.

The Indians had position on the side and top of the mountain and the troops were on the bank of a small stream below. With horse the Indians could not be reached. They therefore had to dismount only having a few men to guard the horses. The troops ascended the mountain, drove the Indians from their position but lost five men killed.

The Indians were in great force, had the troops surrounded and made an attempt to secure their horses, but, by the timely arrival of Davidson, they failed. The Indians were firing on the troops from every direction. They could not be seen (as they) were concealed behind trees in the brush.

The troops charged them several times but those whom they charged would retreat and join those in the rear. Finding that it was impossible to do any execution on account of the situation in which he was placed and having lost several men in killed and wounded, he was compelled to retreat though reluctantly on his part but the officer with him and seeing the deplorable condition of his men caused him to give up the idea of maintaining his position. The retreat was sounded, the Indians in great numbers in pursuit. The troops had to wheel about several times to charge the Indians. They finally succeeded in reaching the main road to Taos but lost in killed twenty two soldiers and nearly every one of the command wounded. The number of Indians killed during that day has never as yet been ascertained but there is no doubt but a great number of them were slain.

I returned to Taos the next day after the fight, having passed near the place where it had been but did not meet an Indian. They had all fled and took a direction across the Del Norte.[62]

On the 4th day of April 1854, Lieutenant Colonel Cooke, 2 Dragoons organized a command for the purpose of pursuing the Indians and giving them sad chastisement as they deserved. He employed a company of forty Pueblo Indians and Mexicans under the command of Mr. James H. Quinn, as Captain and John Mastin as his Lieutenant, they were men in every way qualified to perform the service for which they were employed and that was to proceed some distance in advance of the main body and act as spies and keep the trail of the Indians. I accompanied them on march as principal guide.

The march was taken up on the 4th and reached Arroyo Hondo, some ten miles north of Taos, then took down said stream to where it empties into the Rio Grande, having passed through a deep and difficult cañon for the passage of troops. The Del Norte River was high but it had to be crossed. The bed of the river is full of large rocks and in crossing the

---

62. The Del Norte and the Rio Grande are the same river.

horses would sometimes be only to their knees in the water and then have to step off of a rock. They would be over their backs and would necessarily have some trouble in ascending the next rock.

I took the lead and finally crossed. The troops then commenced their passage and crossed, meeting with no very serious accident more than two or three dragoons were nearly drowned to cross the Infantry (helping the Infantry cross?)

The Dragoon horses had to be recrossed for the purpose of getting them over. It was finally done, I crossing and recrossing the river about twenty times. The command had all crossed. We had now to ascend from the river.

The cañon is at the lowest calculation 600 feet high but by leading the animals cautiously through the different windings of the trail we ascended, continued our march over a plain in which there were many cañons and deep ravines destitute of water and grass till we arrived at Sirvilletta,[63] a small Mexican town, where we encamped and forage was purchased for the animals. Marched in the morning and in two days found the trail, followed it two days and overtook the Indians. They saw us approaching and retreated. They were pursued. Several Indians killed and a number of horses and their camp equipage captured. There was one soldier killed and one wounded.

Captain Sykes, of the Infantry, deserves great praise for his conduct on this march. He was in command of the Infantry. He had a horse with him but

---

63. Not the R. R. town of today but a small plaza near Pataca.

on which I do not think he mounted during the campaign. He would wade the streams, through much ice and snow, often for the distance of ten miles, I really believe, that, by his conduct, the courage of his men was kept up. I could not understand how men were able to undergo such hardships. The marches were generally long, over high mountains covered with snow and not having a sufficiency, the troops were on half rations. They surely would have failed through fatigue and the want of provisions, if they had not had an officer to command them as he did, willingly going through the hardships they all had to undergo and being always in the advance.

When the Indians were seen, he and his company were in the advance of the troops, the spies being some distance ahead of him. But when the word Indians reached him, he and his men raised a run and entered the Indian village in company with the Dragoons. And from his Company the (one) man was killed and one wounded. The Indians were pursued through a deep canyon for about four miles. Many were not seen but the number of killed Indians was seven and a number wounded.

It became dark. The command returned to where the Indians had been encamped and bivouacked for the night. In the morning the wounded man was sent back for the purpose of receiving medical aid and a corporal and a party of privates attended him, as an escort.

The command now took the trail of the Indians, following them through deep cañons over high

mountains covered with snow. They could not be
again overtaken. They were broken up into small
bands. Trails were leading in different directions.
And trails would be followed and at night the command would nearly have to return to the place from
which it marched in the morning.

The Jicarilla Apache Indians are the worst that
are to be pursued. They always, after having been
attacked, retreat in small parties and have no baggage, and are capable of travelling several days without food, that it is impossible for any comdg or regular troops to overtake them if they are aware of their
being pursued.

They were followed six days and the comdg officer finding that they could not be overtaken concluded to march to Abiguiu,[64] a Mexican village situated
on the Chama River (a tributary of the Del Norte)
for the purpose of recruiting his animals. Arrived
about the 14 April.

The party that had returned with the wounded
man met on their march a Utah Indian, took him
prisoner, depriving him of his arms and horse. He
made his escape and joined his tribe.

Col. Cooke, fearing that such treatment given a
friendly Indian by men of his party might cause the
tribe of which he was a member to join the Indians
that were at war. I immediately departed for my
agency at Taos, sent a man to the village of the
Utahs, requesting their head men to come to the
agency, that I wanted to talk to them. In a short

---

64. Abiqui, far from a railroad, is one of the quaintest old hill towns
   in New Mexico and still a stronghold of the sect called Penitentes.

time after my arrival several came and I stated to
them that the soldiers that took one of their tribe
prisoner had done so thinking that he was an Apache;
that the Americans did not wish to do them any injury and that I hoped that they would remain friendly and for them to render no aid to the Indians that
were at war. If they did so, they would be treated
as enemies.

They promised not to render any assistance to
the Apaches. I then returned to them the property
captured and they departed. I remained at the
Agency.

Colonel Cooke, after remaining a few days at
Abiquiu marched in pursuit of the hostile Indians,
followed them several days, was caught in a snow
storm and, the trail being many days old and the
ground covered with snow, it was useless to attempt
to proceed. He then returned to the Rio Colorado.
A reinforcement of troops arrived under command
of Major Brooks 3 Infantry. As soon as the necessary preparations could be made another campaign
was to be made against the enemy.

Colonel Cooke took command of the troops that
had been on the two previous campaign(s) and
marched to Taos. The men of his command were
much worn down by the hardships through which
they had gone and his animals knocked up. All men
and horses required repose. I can say of Colonel
Cooke that he is as efficient an officer to make cam-
paigns against Indians as I ever accompanied, that
he is brave and gallant all know.

Christopher Carson
From a Photograph Taken in Boston, Mass., about Six Months before
His Death. Carson went to Boston to Consult a Physician

The Indians by his persevering pursuit lost many by hardship and the severe cold and if they had not been so fortunate as to have kept the American horse they captured in their fight with Lieut. Davidson, they would not have been enabled to elude him and if they had been caught they would have been chastised in such a manner that war with *that* tribe would never again occur.

Major Brooks and command marched against the Indians, followed their trail for several days, arrived in the Utah country. Finding that the country was entirely cut up with trails and it being impossible to designate the one of the enemy, he was compelled to give up the pursuit and return to Taos. He arrived about the 15 May. Had been in the field some 10 or 15 days and had not the fortune to meet any of the enemy. Done no execution.

Major Carleton, 1 Dragoons, was encamped in Taos making preparations for a campaign. About the 23 May everything was ready. He marched in pursuit of the enemy. I accompanied him as principal guide. We marched north to Fort Massachusetts, then the spies under command of Captain Quinn marched west to the White mountains[65] and thence along its base to the Mosco Pass through to the Huerfano, his object being to discover the trail for the place. Major Brooks gave up the pursuit. It was evident that the Indians were making for the Mosco Pass. The command marched through the Sangre de Cristo Pass, was to join with Captain Quinn on the Huerfano in three days. Both parties joined on the

---

65. The Blanca range near which was situated Fort Massachusetts.

Huerfano.[66] I discovered a trail of three Indians in the Pass, followed it till I came to the main trail near the Huerfano. Quinn discovered (at the entrance) of the Mosco Pass an old encampment of the Indians (at its entrance). They had passed through the Pass as predicted. The main trail was now taken and followed six days when the Indians were discovered. We marched over very rugged country, mountains, cañons, ravines had to be passed, but we overtook the Indians at last. The Indians were encamped in the east side of Fisher's Peak in the Raton mountains.

The troops charged in on the village. The Indians run. Some were killed and about 40 head of horses were captured. They were followed till dark. There was a party of men under command of Lt. R. Johnston I Dragoons, left at the village. Captain Quinn and three of his spies were with him. They concealed themselves in the brush near the village. One of the spies knew the call to be made by those Indians when scattered, sounded it and shortly, two Indians and two squaws made their appearance, were fired upon by the spies and one was killed (an Indian.) Nothing more could be done. The Indians were made aware of the party being near them, by the firing of the gun and the yells of the Indians that made their escape. In the vicinity of the village, the brush was thick and there being many places of concealment, I have no doubt hiding in such places, the Indians saved themselves.

66. Huerfano means orphan and is the name the natives have long given to one small mountain not far from the Spanish Peaks. It stands quite alone.

Then the command marched back for a few miles
and encamped for the night. It was entirely owing
to the good management of Major Carleton that the
Indians were discovered. He directed the spies to
keep the trail. The troops followed but keeping as
much concealed as possible by marching through the
brush and timber. In the morning of the day, that
we overtook the Indians, I saw a trail that was fresh,
informed the Major that, if we met with no accident
that the Indians would be found by two o'clock. He
told me that, if such would be the case, that he would
present me one of the finest hats that could be procured in New York. The Indians were found at the
hour I had predicted. The Major fulfilled his prom-
ise presenting to me a hat, he directed to be made in
New York,—and a fine one it was.

The command now commenced its return for
Taos, travelling to the head waters of the Canadian
and its tributaries. Passed over beautiful though
mountainous country and arrived at Taos in June.
I did not accompany any other campaign for the remainder of the year.

Major Blake I Dragoons made a campaign in
July. Was absent some time but did not find any
of the Indians. In August, I departed from the
Agency to visit the Utahs for the purpose of collect-
ing them to meet the Superintendent at Abiquiu in
October. I had to travel about 200 miles, passing in
the vicinity of a village of Apaches. Passed unper-
ceived by them and arrived at the Utah village. Gave
them the notice that the Superintendent wished to

see them in October. They agreed to go see him. I then departed for the Agency, arrived in a few days.

In October I proceeded to the Council. The Indians attended as promised. Presents were given to them and they appeared friendly. Previous to the Council some Mexicans had killed a Utah Indian for the purpose of getting the coat he wore. The Indians were much dissatisfied requesting animals in payment of the death of the Indian. Animals would not be paid them, but it was promised that the murderers would be arrested and punished according to law. One of the murderers was even apprehended but, in a very short time, made his escape, and nothing more was attempted to be done to render justice to the Indians.

On their way to their hunting grounds the small pox broke out among them. The leading men of the band of Muache Utahs died. They came to the conclusion that the Superintendent was the cause of the disease being among them, that he had collected them for the purpose of injuring them, that to the head men he gave each a blanket coat and that every one that received a coat died, that the coats were the cause of the deaths. The Indians firmly believed and the murderer of the Indians being allowed to escape unpunished and they having but poor faith in anything the Superintendent promised them, they commenced preparing for war. Joined the Apaches and commenced committing depredations. They attacked the settlement of Costilla, killed some men and drove off nearly all the stock, and stole and murdered citizens as they could be found.

The regular troops in the country were not sufficiently strong to make a campaign against the
Utahs when joined with the Apaches.[67] The Governor
issued a proclamation calling for six companies of
volunteers. It was immediately responded to. The
companies were organized. Several companies having offered their services now they was called for,
showing the willingness of the people to enter military service when called upon to punish their enemies. And if the chastisement of the Indians of this
country was left to the citizens, I have no doubt but
that in a short period they would bring them to sub-
jection. As it is at present the Indians are masters
of the country. They commit depredation when they
please. Perhaps a command of troops will be sent
after them. They will be overtaken, some of the
property they stole recovered and they make their
escape unpunished. The superintendent will then
call them in to have a grand talk. Presents are giv-
en, promises are made but only to be broken when
convenient. I can say that this country will always
remain in its improverished state as long as them
mountain Indians are permitted to run at large and
the only remedy is to compel them to live in settlements, cultivate the soil and learn to gain their main-
tenance independent of the general government.

After the organization of the volunteers, the
Governor appointed Captain Ceran St. Vrain of
Taos, as their Commander. He was a gentleman in
every manner qualified for such office, the greater

67. Apaches have the name of being the most murderous of all the
southwestern Indians.

part of his life having been passed in the mountains
and this Territory.

And when the people became aware of the Governor having chosen a man so competent to fulfill
the duties of an office of such importance there was
great rejoicing, for all knew the Captain to be a
gentleman and the bravest of soldiers. And now
were confident that, under the command of such a
man that the Indians would be punished in such a
manner that it would be long before they would
again commence hostilities. In fact, it was the only
appointment of the Governor that met the approba-
tion of the people. Many were surprised at his sound
judgment in making such a noble choice.

In Feb. 1855, Colonel T. T. (J. J.?) Fauntleroy
I Dragoons arrived in Taos, commenced making
preparations to take the field. He had under his
command four companies of Volunteers commanded
by Colonel St. Vrain, two companies of Dragoons,
one of Artillery and one of spies, commanded by
Lucien Stewart of this place, a gentleman that has
passed a great deal of his life in the mountains and
having had a great deal of experience in Indian war-
fare, he was well qualified to perform the duties for
which he was employed.

The command took up its march the fore part of
March, travelled north to Fort Massachusetts,
thence to the Rio Del Norte, up it to where it leaves
the mountain, thence north to the Saquachi Pass,
where the Indians were found in force.

They were attacked, defeated, losing a number in killed and wounded. The artillery was left after the fight at the Saguachi in charge of the train of provisions, Lieutenant Lloyd Beall 2d Arty being in command.

It was (a) very important position and required an officer of judgment and one that did not fear danger to be entrusted with such a duty, and he was the one chosen, and the duty was performed to the satisfaction of the Colonel.

The command now marched in pursuit of the Indians, followed them a few days and, on the head waters of the Arkansas, a large party were discovered. They were immediately charged upon and defeated. Some were killed and many horses were taken. Marched for Fort Massachusetts, passed through the Mosco Pass and arrived the last of March.

The country passed over to Saguachi was level, covered with snow and during the time there were as cold days as ever I experienced. The remainder of the march was over high mountains covered with snow.

I then returned to Taos, the command was distributed in the several settlements so that forage could be procured for the animals, they being in a very reduced condition. Remained (at the) settlements till the middle of April, and started on campaign. I did not accompany this expedition. Colonel T. T. Fauntleroy took a direction the same as on the previous campaign, and travelled to the Punchi Pass, where the Indians were found. Many of them were

killed, a number of animals and camp equipage captured. The Indians were entirely routed. Colonel
St. Vrain marched through the Sangre de Cristo
Pass and on to the Purgatoire River, where the Indians were discovered, attacked, completely routed,
animals and baggage captured. He followed their
trail, had men in pursuit of Indians in every direction. Indians were killed daily, women taken prisoners. On that campaign the Apaches received chastisement for their many depredations, that they
thought could never have been given them. The commands returned to Taos.

Fauntleroy did not again take the field. The
Volunteers had but a short period to serve but St.
Vrain did not allow them to be idle. He immediately
again took the field, and kept in pursuit of Indians
till a few days before the expiration of service. If
the Volunteers had continued in the service three
months and had (been) under the command and sole
direction of Colonel St. Vrain, there would never
again have (been) need (of) any troops in this country. The Indians would be entirely subjected and, in
all probability, but a few of them would be left to be
of any trouble. But such was not the case. Those
in power considered the Indians sufficiently punished; the Indians asked for peace, it was granted
them.

The Superintendent made, in August, treaties
with the Indians that had not been at war. In September the hostile Indians came in, received presents
and promised future friendship.

Facsimile of the Original Manuscript
Courtesy of the Newberry Library, Chicago, Ill.

The Apaches did not all come in at the time of the treaty. They were committing depredations. This fact was reported to the Superintendent but would not be believed. Treaty should not have been made with the Apaches. No faith can be placed in their promises.

The Indians were promised certain sums yearly in case they wished to settle on some stream and commence farming; they had their choice of country.

The Superintendent went to Washington with his treaties which were laid before the Senate and as yet (have) not been confirmed. They should not. Such treaties were not of a character to suit the people. The Apaches are now daily committing depredations. They go unp(un)ished and in my opinion, ere long, they may again commence hostilities. The other tribes with whom the treaties were made, I think will comply with their demands and will not again be hostile if the Government does not stop their supplies of provisions during such times as they cannot hunt.

I frequently visit the Indians, speak to them of the advantages of peace and use my influence with them to keep them satisfied with the proceedings of those placed in power over them. I attended September 4th, 1856 at the assembly of Indians at Abiquiu held by the Superintendent for the purpose of giving them presents. They appeared to be content, then there was a disturbance. The next day a Tabaguachi Utah tore up the blanket given him. It was old, had been worn and he was dissatisfied. He wished to kill the Superintendent but was hindered by the other Indians. I cannot see how the Superintendent can expect Indians to depart satisfied (that) he has called (them) to see him from a distance of 2 or 3 hundred miles, compelled (them) to go several days without anything to eat, unless they have carried it with them.

They are given a meal by the Superintendent, then the presents are given. Some get a blanket; those, that get none, are given a knife or hatchet or some vermillion, a piece of red or blue cloth, some sugar and perhaps a few more trinkets. They could more than earn the quantity they receive in one day's hunt if left in their own country. They could procure skins and furs and traders could furnish the same articles to them and they would be saved the necessity of coming such a distance, thereby not causing their animals to be fatigued and themselves have to travel without food.

If presents are given them it should be taken to their country. They should not be allowed to come into the settlements, for every visit an Indian makes to a town, it is of more or less injury to him.

I am now living in Taos, N. M. in the discharge of my official duties as Indian Agent. Am daily visited by the Indians, give to them presents, as directed by the Superintendent. I am opposed to the policy of having Indians come to the settlements but as no agency buildings are allowed to be built in the country of the Indians, necessity compels them to come to the towns.

The foregoing I hereby transfer to Mr. Jesse B. Truly[68] to be used as he may deem proper for our Joint benefit.

Signed (In Carson's handwriting)

C. CARSON

---

68. Jesse B. Truly was probably the Jesu or Jesse B. Turley whose name is found in early Taos records. He probably was a notary public.

TEN YEARS MORE

So ran the story of his life as Carson told it seventy years ago. There were yet to pass ten years before the call to the Great Beyond. In May, 1868, stricken with trouble caused by a fall from his horse, some time before, he was taken to Fort Lyon, Colorado. Weary days went by and finally, one afternoon, while he was listening to his friend Alois Scheurich, he suddenly turned and said, "Doctor, compadre, adios!" and was gone.

During these last ten years he was constantly thoughtful of his red friends. The older he grew the more his heart went out to worthy Indians and the more he wanted to do for them. He had little use for the Indian who, at that late day, remained hostile.

The days of the Civil War found him fighting the Navajos. It is true that this tribe of Indians suffered terribly at that time but to blame Carson for this as some have who never really studied the causes for the trouble of those days is far, very far from fair. To the honest student of Carson's whole life, not merely of those war years, there comes no proof of deliberate wrong-doing. There is not the slightest cause to call him a "bandit" as some uninformed men have done. There is nowhere any proof that he ever killed wantonly. In California, we know, there are those who recall the killing of the De Herrara boys and blame Carson. Of this, a California historian recently said, "If Carson fired the shots that killed those three who, during war time, were landing where they had no right to go, it was *because he was acting under orders.*" No! There is no blot on the escutcheon of the Taos scout.

Carson lived in the day when the hostile Indian had to be met in battle. His duty was clear. He never shirked. Ever courageous he played the part of a real man. He won his title of Brevet Brigadier General by sheer force of character and ability. The more one studies the life of the famous scout the more profoundly does he proclaim him, a great man. Like most or all great men, he had his faults, of course, but they are hard to discover at this late date.

Little men who knew him as he came and went in old Taos thought of him lightly perhaps because they did not know what Carson had done or was doing. He went about his business in a quiet unassuming manner. So we have one old-timer saying he was "overestimated" and further announcing that he is much surprised that the Americans of today make so much of Carson. Were our opinion of Carson built on the word of this late day it would merit little credence. Such is not the case. It is based solidly on what men of importance said about Carson when he was still *living*. Could such men as Col. J. C. Fremont, Gen. James Rusling, Lt. G. D. Brewerton, Gen. W. T. Sherman, as well as practically every man who wrote of the west in those days, have been mistaken in their estimate of the scout? In every record, one finds evidence of the same deep respect and even love for the small, wiry, silent man who acted and never boasted.

Probably all the true stories about Carson have been told by others and it is not necessary to retell them. There are many that show his love and loyalty to his home and his kindness to Indians in trouble who sought him as "Father Kit." There seems to be but one which has never been caught on the press. This is one Teresina Bent Scheurich, his niece, used to tell.

After the death of her father Gov. Bent in 1847, Carson took the little Teresina to live in his home. He did all he could for his bright-eyed niece. Years went by and school days both in Taos and Santa Fé were over. The girl was a charming young woman of eighteen. She was staying with her uncle on his ranch farm over the mountains in the Rayado. Toward night a large group of Indians surrounded the house. They demanded food. Supper was soon ready. It was Teresina's part to pour the coffee. Timidly she went the rounds of the table. Suddenly her shaking hands let fall the coffee pot. No wonder! She saw the dark eyes of a young Indian fixed upon her and glow deeper and deeper as he looked. She slipped away into the kitchen shaking with fear.

When the supper was finally over, the young Indian sought out Carson and demanded that he give him the young Teresina as his bride. Carson protested that he had no right to do so, and that he would have to consult the girl's mother. Meantime his mind was working quickly for he knew these Indians were none too friendly and was fearful lest they take the matter into their own hands. He parleyed with them. He gave them presents and once back in the house barracaded the doors, assuring the frightened girl that he would kill her and himself before he would allow her to fall into the hands of the Indians. The night of anxious waiting wore away. Morning brought relief. The Indians were gone.

Carson knew well that the Indians were probably not far away. He knew too that there were not enough men on the ranch to resist the Indians for long in case of an attack. So he decided on the seemingly rash course of calling for his horses and hurrying with the women of the household quickly through the cañon back to the Taos home. Even here the Indian sought her out again, only to learn that, under no circumstances, could the pretty Teresina Bent be his bride. She was safe among friends and away went the unwelcome dusky suitor.

Mrs. Scheurich often told this story to her friends, among whom was a Mrs. Henry Craig, widow of a Colonel in the army. She could match the story for as a young woman she had been sought also by a visiting Indian who asked the young army man what he would take for his fair bride. He laughingly told the redskin that nothing short of forty ponies would do. The hours of only one night passed when suddenly there was a great stamping in the street. The Indian had come and with him the forty ponies! Then it was no easy matter for the young bridegroom to convince the dark-eyed suitor that no number of ponies or cattle could buy from him his precious wife.

There is no one now living in Taos or vicinity who knew Carson well or there would be other tales to tell no doubt. Certain it is, that all the old-time stories reveal the character of the great Taos scout as a man ever ready to assist the weak or distressed, a man who forced respect for law, a man who carried throughout life a reputation for honesty, the modern man might well covet, a man who deserved what Fremont said of him, "With me Carson and the truth are the same thing."

Teresina Bent Scheurich
Daughter of Governor Charles Bent and Niece of Kit Carson

WHAT CONTEMPORARIES WROTE
ABOUT CARSON

Gen. W. T. Sherman wrote:

"I well remember the first overland mail. It was brought by Kit Carson in saddle bags from Taos in New Mexico. We heard of his arrival at Los Angeles, and waited patiently for his arrival at headquarters. His fame then was at its height, from the publication of Fremont's books, and I was very anxious to see a man who had achieved such feats of daring among the wild animals of the Rocky Mountains and still wilder Indians of the Plains. At last his arrival was reported at the tavern at Monterey, and I hurried to hunt him up. I cannot express my surprise at beholding a small, stoop-shouldered man, with reddish hair, freckled face, soft blue eyes, and nothing to indicate extraordinary courage or daring. He spoke but little, and answered questions in monosyllables. I asked for his mail, and he picked up his light saddle-bags containing the great overland mail, and we walked together to headquarters, where he delivered his parcel unto Colonel Mason's own hands. He spent some days in Monterey, during which we extracted with difficulty some items of his personal history. He was then by commission a lieutenant in the regiment of Mounted Rifles serving in Mexico under Colonel Summer, and, as he could not reach his regiment from California, Colonel Mason ordered that for a time he should be assigned to duty with

A. J. Smith's company, First Dragoons, at Los Angeles. He remained at Los Angeles some months, and was then sent back to the United States with dispatches, traveling two thousand miles almost alone, in preference to being encumbered by a large party." Memoirs of General W. T. Sherman pp. 46-47.—1849.

* * * * * * * * *

Capt. Chas. A. Montgomery wrote:

"A man old in years but erect and strong on his feet came toward me with extended hand and told me I was welcome. The man was Kit Carson, who guided John C. Fremont on his pathfinding journey across the mountains and plains of what was then an unknown territory of the United States. Carson was the one man that was thought of by the white men living east of the Mississippi river as knowing more about the Indian of the West and Southwest than any other man alive up to that date. To describe him physically is easy. A small, compact, well-proportioned body, weighing about one hundred and thirty-five pounds; five feet six inches in height; gray eyes that looked into yours with honesty and strength—a characteristic of the man. My impression was that I had met my master, one who could teach me what I wanted to know; and so it proved, for during the two weeks I spent as his guest I received advice and instruction, followed out as far as circumstances would allow, that carried me through a rather checkered life on the frontier from the Arkansas river to the Rio Colorado.

Mr. Carson was an uneducated man, but nature had equipped him with brains to plan his work and nerve and judgment to execute the same; and in his time and country he was a great power for good as the white man interprets the word. To me he was a friend never to be forgotten. So clear and vivid was his description of the route he laid out for me to take to reach a friend of his who was to direct my schooling that I missed Fort Richardson, the objective point, four hundred miles away, by only forty miles, striking the Salt Fork of the Brazos river just forty miles west of the fort. The journey to that post on the northeastern frontier of Texas took me through a country then unknown to the white man. My living to make the trip was of some value to the military commanders of the lower country.

But of that fact Mr. Carson did not live to be told. The next summer he passed away, leaving a record excelled by no man of his calling, and a memory, with those who had the good fortune to know him, that will remain fresh and green while life may last. My one wish is that in the life hereafter I may mix with him again. 1867—Sunset Magazine, March, 1911.

* * * * * * * *

J. H. Widber, a pioneer of 1849, says in a still unpublished manuscript in the Bancroft Library:

"Carson was a small man, very wiry, and about as ready an appearing man as I ever saw. He looked as if he would know exactly what to do, if awakened suddenly in the night, ready for anything that might turn up at any moment."

James Madison Cutts in his book "The Conquest of California and New Mexico" published in 1847, wrote:

"Under this name (Kit Carson), within a few years, has become quite familiar to the public, mainly through his connection with the expeditions of Fremont, one of the best of those noble and original characters that have from time to time sprung up on and beyond our frontier, retreating with it to the west, and drawing from association with uncultivated nature, not the rudeness and sensualism of the savage, but genuine simplicity and truthfulness of disposition, and generosity, bravery, and single-heartedness to a degree rarely found in society.—He has been celebrated (though now aged only thirty-seven years) as a hunter, trapper, guide, or pilot of the prairies, and Indian fighter, uniting to the necessary characteristics of that adventurous and sturdy class, a kindness of heart and gentleness of manner that relieves it of any possible harshness or asperity."

* * * * * * * *

Brig. Gen. Carleton in an order to Carson during the Civil War, wrote:

"Much is expected of you both here and in Washington."

* * * * * * * *

Mrs. Jessie Benton Fremont, wife of the famous explorer, in an interview about thirty years ago, an account of which was given in "The Land of Sunshine" Feb. 1897, said:

Col. Dick Rutledge
The Last of the Old Scouts, at the Grave of Kit Carson. 1924.
H. E. High

"Kit Carson was a man among men, a type of the real American pioneer, not only fearless but clear-headed, as gentle as he was strong. He had the true courtesy of the heart, and withal a quiet pride—much as Richard the Lion-Heart and his knights, who thanked God they were not clerks.—His nature was literally sweet, sweet by its wholesomeness—sweet as a clear-cut winter morning is sweet.

Later speaking of Carson's visit to the Fremont home in St. Louis, she said:

"Carson was shy and reserved and his welcome as one who had been Fremont's companion and right-hand man overwhelmed him. Yet he was not awkward. A perfect gentleman, his dignity and delicacy completely disarmed my mother. He had been afraid the ladies might not care to have him there if they knew he had married a Sioux wife. 'But she was a good woman,' he declared. 'I never came in from hunting but she had warm water for my feet.' I have always remembered that—it was so like the simplicity of the Bible.

There was an illustrated edition of Byron in the parlor and in it one day Carson came upon the steel engraving of Mazeppa and began to see what it meant.

'Read it to me!' he cried at last. 'You can read so much faster. So I read to him. He walked up and down, intensely stirred.

'There never yet was human power
That could evade, if unforgiven,
The patient search, and vigil long,
Of him who treasures up a wrong.'

'That's it! That's the word!' he broke out. 'He knows how it is! It took me three years before I could go back and *thank* those Blackfeet for robbing my caches.' After this, I had to read 'Mazeppa' nearly every day."

* * * * * * * * *

James F. Meline, gives the following, in a letter from Santa Fé under date of August 11, 1866,

"The pleasantest episode of my visit here has been the society of Kit Carson, with whom I passed three days. I need hardly say delightfully. He is one of the few men I ever met who can talk long hours to you of what he has seen and yet say very little about himself. He has to be drawn out. I had many questions to ask and his answers were all marked by great distinctness of memory, simplicity, candor, and a desire to make some one else, rather than himself, the hero of his story."

* * * * * * * * *

Col. Henry Inman wrote:

"Kit's nature was composed of the noblest attributes; he was brave, but never reckless like Custer, unselfish, a veritable exponent of Christian altruism; and as true to his friends as steel to the magnet."—1897

* * * * * * * * *

Lt. G. D. Brewerton said he wished to offer his "humble testimony to the sterling worth of a man, who I am proud to say was my guide, companion and friend through some of the wildest regions ever traversed by the foot of man."—1848.

Gen. James F. Rusling, in his "Across Ameri-
ca" 1857, quotes Gen. W. T. Sherman as saying:

"These red skins think Kit twice as big a man as
me. Why, his integrity is simply perfect. They (the
Utes) know it and they would believe him and trust
him any day before me."

Later Rusling said of Carson:

"He impressed you at once as a man of rare
kindliness and charity such as a truly brave man
ought always to be. As simple as a child but as
brave as a lion he soon took our hearts by storm and
grew upon our regard all the while we were with
him."

* * * * * * * * *

Assistant Surgeon H. R. Tilton of the U. S.
Army was with Carson when he died at Fort Lyon,
Colorado. In a letter under date of January 7th,
1874, he wrote to the author John S. C. Abbott, the
following:

"It was wonderful to read of the stirring scenes,
thrilling deeds and narrow escapes, (referring to
Peter's Life of Carson) and then look at the quiet,
modest, retiring, but dignified little man who has
done so much.

You are perfectly correct in describing Carson
as a gentleman. He was one of nature's nobleman—
a true man in all that constitutes manhood—pure—
honorable—truthful—sincere—of noble impulses, a
true knight-errant ever ready to defend the weak
against the strong, without reward other than his
own conscience.

Carson had great contempt for noisy braggarts and shams of every sort.

Carson was made a brigadier-general of volunteers by brevet, at the close of the rebellion.

Shortly after coming to my quarters he made his will, and left property to the value of seven thousand dollars to his children.

I have been this minute, thinking that, while writing his life, you had grown to love him, as all who knew him certainly cherished great affection for him.''

* * * * * * * * *

The following letter which appeared in the Army and Navy Journal in 1860 must be given here to complete the story of the famous Taos scout. His close friend and biographer, Col. D. C. Peters, wrote as follows:

Sir:

On the 23rd day of May, 1868, at Fort Lyon C. T. (Colorado Territory) died General Christopher Carson, late of the U. S. Volunteers. It was my fortune to have known Kit Carson intimately for a number of years. He even dictated his life to me which I endeavored to write but I fear I failed in faithfully portraying his exploits and character to his credit. Kit Carson was born in 1809 in Kentucky and emigrated with his father's family to Missouri at an early age. In 1825, he started with some trappers for the then unknown Rocky Mountains by the ''Santa Fé Trail.'' He soon became a leader of these

Kit Carson III and Kit Carson IV

hunters and traders and from the Columbia River of the north to the Rio Grande, he rose to renown. His bravery, high-toned honour, integrity and simplicity of character soon became known. He was the truest and best friend the red men of the West ever had, and yet in war he was their worst enemy. Appointed a lieutenant in the U. S. Rifles, when that regiment was organized, he was stationed in California, but not being confirmed by the U. S. Senate, he resigned and returned to New Mexico, his chosen home where he has lived a most exemplary and active life. No man ever lived who has performed more feats of daring among the Indian race than Kit Carson.

His last and greatest act was in subjugating some 8000 Navajo Indians and compelling them to settle on a reservation.

He combined all the tact and ingenuity of our great frontiermen and pioneers like Daniel Boone, David Crockett, and others. His name in the old army was legion, and I am positive that many a tear will be shed by his old friends in the army and elsewhere when it is known that he is no more. New Mexico has lost one of its choicest citizens and most gallant men. He sleeps but his name is identified with every great achievement in civilization in this rocky chain of mountains.

General Carson had recently returned home an invalid, after a mission of charity in behalf of the Utah and Apache Indians. His wife died a short time previous to his demise, and the shock was too

great for him. He died suddenly although not un-
expectedly of the rupture of a blood vessel, at the
quarters of the post Surgeon of Fort Lyon, C. T.
having received every kindness his great and good
heart deserved. A better, braver, a more honest and
warmer friend never lived. Peace be to his ashes.

D. C. PETERS,
Brevet Lieutenant Colonel and Surgeon, U. S. A.
Fort Union, New Mexico, May 26, 1868.

Printed in the United States
117944LV00005B/151/A